Mortal Dilemmas

Mortal Dilemmas

The Troubled Landscape
of Death in America

Donald Joralemon

Walnut Creek, California

LEFT COAST PRESS, INC.
1630 North Main Street, #400
Walnut Creek, CA 94596
www.LCoastPress.com

Copyright © 2016 by Left Coast Press, Inc.

ISBN 978-1-62958-392-1 hardback
ISBN 978-1-62958-393-8 paperback
ISBN 978-1-62958-394-5 institutional eBook
ISBN 978-1-62958-395-2 consumer eBook

Library of Congress Cataloging-in-Publication Data:

Names: Joralemon, Donald.
Title: Mortal dilemmas : the troubled landscape of death in America / Donald Joralemon.
Description: Walnut Creek, CA : Left Coast Press, 2016.
Identifiers: LCCN 2015035205| ISBN 9781629583921 (hardback) | ISBN 9781629583938
(paperback) | ISBN 9781629583945 (institutional ebook) | ISBN 9781629583952 (consumer
eBook)
Subjects: LCSH: Death—Social aspects—United States. | Grief—Social aspects—United
States. | BISAC: SOCIAL SCIENCE / General. | SOCIAL SCIENCE / Death & Dying. | SOCIAL
SCIENCE / Anthropology / Cultural.
Classification: LCC HQ1073.5.U6 J67 2016 | DDC 306.90973—dc23
LC record available at http://lccn.—loc.gov/2015035205

Printed in the United States of America

∞™ The paper used in this publication meets the minimum requirements of American
National Standard for Information Sciences—Permanence of Paper for Printed Library
Materials, ANSI/NISO Z39.48–1992.

Contents

List of Abbreviations

ANH: artificial nutrition and hydration

DNR: do not resuscitate order

DSM: Diagnostic and Statistical Manual of the American Psychiatric Association

DOI: Department of the Interior, United States

ICD: International Classification of Disease, World Health Organization

MDD: major depressive disorder

NAGPRA: Native American Graves Protection and Repatriation Act

PAD: physician-assisted death

PEG: percutaneous endoscopic gastrostomy

PCBD: persistent complex bereavement disorder

PGD: prolonged grief disorder

PVS: permanent or persistent vegetative state

UDDA: Uniform Death Determination Act

UNOS: United Network for Organ Sharing

VS: vegetative state

Acknowledgments

Friends, colleagues, and students deserve recognition for helping me with this project. Reyes Lazaro suggested the main title, Christina Staudt read and commented on an earlier draft and invited me to talk to the Columbia University Seminar on Death, Dr. Audrey Pendleton provided a physician's view on an earlier draft, George Dickenson provided especially helpful observations, and many online readers contributed useful ideas. I have had able research assistance from several Smith College students: Katherine Russell, Chloe Vaughn, Victoria von Saucken, Ana Sofia Moreno-Mesa, and Katilyn Marasi.

Parts of Chapter 1 appeared in a previously published article, "Dying While Living: The Problem of Social Death," in Staudt and Ellens (2014).

Prologue

My First Corpse

I was over forty when I saw my first corpse. At a wake on a New Hampshire farm the body was laid out in a homemade coffin in the living room of the old house. The dead woman had been a Catholic nun, then a wife, and finally a state representative; cancer took her at too early an age, her early fifties. Her husband, an eccentric Ukrainian who prided himself on his frugal and ecologically minded lifestyle, had prepared the body, crafted the simple pine coffin, and dug the grave in a field across the road. He told us how he had acquired an undertaker's metal table on which he had washed the body and drained its fluids. He had purchased large quantities of dry ice to slow the process of decomposition, knowing, though, that the ice cream supply company might look askance at the project for which cooling was required. The dehydrated body was shrunken, gray, and cold. It barely resembled the woman I had known.

The next day we assembled for the burial, forming a large circle around the grave and listening to her family and closest friends talk about the life just ended. Musicians performed Irish music in honor of the deceased's ethnic roots. We were invited to shovel dirt into the hole before the family finished the job. Food was served under a tent. Conversation was difficult.

How did I live so long without seeing death incarnate? Most societies, including ours at earlier times, couldn't shelter members from direct encounters with the dead because people died where you had to notice, in the upstairs bedroom

Mortal Dilemmas: The Troubled Landscape of Death in America, by Donald Joralemon, 11–13. © 2016 Left Coast Press, Inc. All rights reserved.

or in plain sight in public spaces. Most of my dead up to that point, including four grandparents and my father, had simply disappeared, whisked away to the crematorium by relatives who saw no point in having family assemble to mark a passing. (In only one instance did I even attend a memorial service, for the internment of a maternal grandmother's ashes in Arlington Cemetery, arranged long after death because of the military services' busy schedule.)

It's perfectly possible that my late introduction to the viewing of corpses is explained by the idiosyncrasies of my family, that there is no general lesson to be learned from my experience. However, thanatologists—scholars who study dying and death—have long argued that over the course of the twentieth century America has increasingly become a society that denies death a public presence by isolating the dying in hospitals and nursing homes and by engaging in ever-more abbreviated and secularized funeral activities. These specialists would expect Americans to be sheltered from any direct exposure to the discomfiting reality of death, just as I had been until I reached middle age.

How do we reconcile the idea that America tries to deny death with the fact that my New Hampshire friends orchestrated a symbolically powerful funeral, corpse included? No good death deniers would go to all that trouble. Perhaps there are some ethnic or religious enclaves in America that have yet to jump on the denial bandwagon, or maybe the "American way of death" is more complicated than historians, social scientists, and the legions of grief counselors would have us believe.

These questions seemed to relate to research I was conducting on the meaning of bodies in the context of organ transplantation. I wanted to know how potential donor families respond to the diagnosis of "brain death," applied to patients on life-support machinery that creates the impression of a living person peacefully sleeping. I also studied proposals to increase the supply of transplantable organs by offering financial incentives for these vital replacement parts. I asked whether American culture had come to accept a radically new way of defining death, based on technological criteria that label the apparently alive as certainly deceased, and whether the bodies of the dead had become property to be bought and sold to the highest bidder.

How do these cultural developments of late twentieth-century America relate to this society's purported tendency to deny death by isolating the dying, minimizing funeral rituals, and limiting the expression and duration of grief? And what does it mean to go against these trends? These are the questions that brought me to the current book.

Points of Contention

I don't intend this book to be an encyclopedic survey of death customs and visions of the afterlife through human history. Scholars from many fields have written both sweeping accounts and particular studies of cultural traditions related to death; there's no need for me to add to this voluminous collection. Instead, I focus my attention on five important areas of contention surrounding dying and death in contemporary America: the right of the dying to end their lives voluntarily, the appropriate treatment of persons in vegetative states, the definition of the boundary between life and death, the repackaging of grief as disease, and the politics of memorials. Taken together, these conflict points contribute to what I call the troubled landscape of death in America. In each instance I ask what the debates that swirl around these topics tell us about how our views of death respond to wider societal changes, from technological innovations to shifts in the American political landscape. At the end I return to the question of death denial by asking: What do these death disputes indicate about how Americans manage mortality, now and into the future?

The issues I address are weighty, and for some readers they will hit close to home. I don't lay claim to answers—the best I can do is clarify what's at stake—and I certainly don't present this book as a therapeutic resource. Self-help sections of every bookstore in the United States have an overabundance of guides intended to assist the dying and comfort the survivors. I'm an academic, not a counselor, and I write to stimulate thought, not to prescribe treatment.

Chapter 1

A Culturally Naked Death?[1]

> Death had been a public and communal event; now it became private. Events that had been part of people's ordinary lives were placed under the control of professionals. The deathbed was moved from home to hospital. Funerals became more discrete; the customary signs of mourning all but disappeared. The prevailing attitude toward death began to be described as "forbidden death," "invisible death," and "death denied." (DeSpelder and Stickland 2002, 50)

At some point in the early twentieth century Americans lost their capacity to perpetuate the collective rituals long associated with dying and death. At least that's the conventional wisdom. Like Tolstoy's Ivan Ilyich, we're condemned to experience a profoundly private death, isolated from relatives and friends who consider dying a serious social embarrassment and inconvenience. According to the French historian Philippe Ariès, the modern obsession with individualism and the promotion of secular views have stripped us of our capacity to create a community around the dying and to share in each other's mourning. Dying is transformed into illness, and, in Ariès's words, an "untamed death" is made invisible.

There certainly is evidence for the claim that much has changed in the way dying and death are managed in modern America. In 1900 only one in five deaths occurred in hospitals or other medical establishments; currently three of four deaths are in hospitals and nursing homes. Of the sixty-five hundred Americans who die every day, nearly five thousand end their lives in a health care environment, where they run up the highest medical costs of their lives during their final hours.

The timing and primary causes of death have also dramatically changed. Over the course of the past hundred years infant mortality and sudden/unexpected deaths have declined, whereas deaths due to progressive diseases and chronic conditions, both of which disproportionately affect persons in later life, have dramatically increased. In 1900 the average life expectancy was forty-nine years; by the end of the century we were closing in on eighty. The top four causes of death in 2010—heart disease, cancer, chronic lower respiratory disease, strokes—accounted for 54 percent of all deaths; these same conditions represented only 15 percent of deaths in 1900. The typical dying person today is elderly, confined in a medical institution, and suffering from the final stages of a chronic illness most often associated with the circulatory and respiratory systems.

Unlike many analysts, I am reluctant to accept at face value the idea that America has become a death-denying culture in need of remedial lessons in more meaningful death customs. It is best to be cautious about generalizations meant to cover "American" dying and death practices. The cultural diversity of America requires us to ask how well the death-denying characterization fits with the many distinct ethnic traditions within this society. Are Mexican Americans death deniers when they build home altars to their deceased and celebrate the Day of the Dead with picnics in graveyards? Are traditional jazz funerals for African Americans in New Orleans or the seven days of mourning (Shiva) among Jews examples of private, invisible deaths? Let's hold the denial theme at arm's length as we consider what can be said in general terms about the management of dying and death in contemporary America.

Social and Biological Death

One development related to death in America that *can* reliably be said to have affected the population as a whole is the degree of medical attention that currently accompanies the end of life. The romantic ideal of the family in quiet attendance at the bedside of the dying person has been largely supplanted by intensive-care units with humming life-support technology—respirators and resuscitators, monitoring devices and crash carts. Cartoonists have captured the irony of a patient almost invisible among the technological apparatus that sustains biological systems (see Figure 1.1).

"I GIVE UP. WHERE'S THE PATIENT?"

Figure 1.1
Used by permission, Cartoonstock.com

The import of this "medicalized" dying is easier to understand if we explore the distinction between social and biological death. The latter refers to the process by which critical organ systems permanently cease to function, and decay and decomposition begin. Life-support technology has made it more difficult than ever to determine with certainty when biological death has occurred, but the concept is at least intuitively sensible. The notion of social death is more complicated; it refers to the disintegration and disappearance of a person's social identity.

Think of yourself as a thread in a network of social relations, linked to others by connections of varying intensity and duration. Taken together, these bonds constitute your social identity and have a profound effect on your own self-image. When you die, there is a tear in the web to which you were connected. The repair of the network requires a reorganization of the bonds without you, or at least without your ongoing engagement. A person with minimal connections, such as a hermit, poses little difficulty to the social system, but people with far-reaching bonds pose a greater recuperative challenge. In either case the concept of social death refers to the process by which the deceased is taken out of the social network altogether or reconfigured so as to perpetuate at least some of the importance of the decedent to the still living (e.g., through memorials, annual death recognitions, beliefs in ghosts).

Through most of human history biological death preceded social death because most people died young and quickly. Funerals were elaborate in part because they bore the burden of repairing the social fabric when an unanticipated death ruptured the network of social relations. But the pattern of longer lives and slower deaths that evolved over the twentieth century in wealthy countries reversed the order: social death first, biological death some time later. Prolonged dying at advanced ages results in the separation of people from their social networks well in advance of biological death. Retirement parties start the process; "to retire," after all, means to withdraw or go away or apart. Eventual moves to assisted-living facilities and then full-care nursing homes nearly complete a person's segregation from society before death. Our social universe narrows in an inexorable movement toward detachment.

The active elderly may protest that they remain fully engaged in life, and aging baby boomers are not likely to go quietly off to seclusion in aged ghettos. But the culturally scripted paths available even to the most energetic seniors—volunteer work, travel, age-adjusted sports, and continuing education—are still steps away from the world of younger people. More time is spent in the exclusive company of persons similarly situated in the life cycle. Social Security, Medicare, geriatric care, and senior discounts increasingly define daily life. For those who survive beyond the statistical mean for their gender and ethnicity, the sense of a shrinking social universe is intensified by the progressive loss of close friends and relatives.

Because so much of the societal work of recuperation from a person's demise is now accomplished before biological death, there is often an anticlimatic character to life's final end. The throttling back of funeral customs is partly explained by the simple fact that funerals have less to accomplish when the dead have already been written out of the social script. Rather than bemoaning this development as an impoverishment of culture, we should stop searching for traditionally elaborate funeral rituals and consider what is taking their place.

Narratives of Social Death

People have always made stories about the things that matter to them. Contemporary literature includes tales about dying that respond to modern mortality patterns and the dilemma of a social death that precedes the biological end of life. Whether fictional or based in the experiences of real people, the majority of the stories detail long-term suffering and medical struggles related to progressive diseases, most notably cancers and neurodegenerative conditions. Some are heroic testimonials to the strength of the human will to battle mortality, complete with moral lessons about living life fully. Others offer sad scenes of lonely people facing painful ends in sterile settings, precautionary tales of the "bad death" for those who, by fault of character, failed to cultivate ties to persons who might have cared.

The archetype of the heroic story is Mitch Albom's *Tuesdays with Morrie* (1997), a sports writer's poignant retelling of his favorite professor's "last class" on the meaning of life and death. After seeing Brandeis sociology professor Morrie Schwartz on the Ted Koppel television program *Frontline,* Albom reconnected with his old mentor over a series of Tuesday meetings that lasted until Morrie died from amyotrophic lateral sclerosis (ALS, or Lou Gehrig's disease). Morrie's willingness to discuss openly and with humor what it feels like to die slowly, together with his life-affirming advice to his former student, is so compelling that ten years after its publication the book had sold over 11 million copies worldwide and had been made into a television movie, starring Jack Lemmon as the dying professor.

There is, however, more to Albom's book than Morrie's clever remarks (e.g., "When you're in bed, you're dead") and pithy axioms ("When you learn how to die, you learn how to live"). The professor's decline also sets the standards for the modern social death. There are the requisite moments of anger, denial, bargaining, depression, and acceptance that Elizabeth Kübler-Ross insisted are critical stages in coming to terms with dying. Then there's a scripted departure from the living community, Morrie's extended review of his life and his predeath funeral with friends and family. By the time Morrie actually dies, most of the work of disengagement from the social fabric has been accomplished, making complicated postmortem rituals largely unnecessary.

Margaret Edson's highly acclaimed play *Wit* (1999) offers the dark opposite of this plotline for social death. Vivian Bearing, a savagely intelligent professor of English literature, is diagnosed with advanced ovarian cancer. The only treatment available to her is an experimental massive course of chemotherapy, which causes her such extreme suffering that she wonders which is worse, the disease or the therapy. Vivian's personality, cold and critical, has left her virtually alone just when she is most in need of the kindness of close relations. Her doctors treat her as a medical subject, reduced to the statistics reported on her medical chart, and provide no sympathy as she tries to endure the brutal assault of chemical poisons on her body. Only an elderly former teacher and her nurse show Vivian any real compassion as she progresses toward the modern nightmare death, in a hospital room being tormented by medical staff attempting an unwanted resuscitation.

Edson gives Vivian ample opportunity to reflect on her life as it comes to a close, but unlike Morrie's life review, hers leads to profound regrets about her inability to connect with other people and her failure to understand the importance of simple human warmth. There is no gathering of loved ones to signify that her life mattered, no indication that her demise will leave so much as a ripple in the world she inhabited. The only redemption is a final insight into the link between living well and dying well. If Morrie offers a model to emulate, Vivian offers a cautionary tale.

The principal characters in these two works focus our attention on the unique opportunity provided by modern conditions of dying, namely that many people now can participate in the social process by which the dying self is disentangled from the cumulative network of relations that define identity. Someone like Morrie, who is embedded in a dense network of relationships with others, faces a very different set of choices from an individual like Vivian, who approaches death as a largely independent and autonomous actor. The fact that there are both Morries and Vivians in our world reminds us to avoid blanket characterizations of social death in contemporary society.

The Liminality of Social Death

Both Morrie and Vivian are enacting modern rituals of dying and death. Anthropologists pay a great deal of attention to such rituals, as they do to all passages that mark an individual's life, such as birth, puberty, and marriage. Studies of these passage rites conclude that they invariably have a period of "liminality," when the individual undergoing the transition from one status to another is, in the words of the anthropologist Victor Turner, "betwixt and between." No longer of the former status but not yet fully situated in the new position, the ritual subject stands temporarily outside the social system. It is common for this liminal period to include the seclusion of the ritual subject, a leveling of social distinctions, a temporary suspension of time, and restrictions on behavior that underscore the ambiguous condition of the person undergoing the transition. In the case of death rituals it is often both the deceased and his/her close kin that are taken through a passage, the former toward the world of the dead and the latter back into the social world after the stigma of association with death is diminished.

In traditional death studies the notion of liminality is used to explain practices that occur between biological death and the final disposition of the corpse, the time period when the deceased has yet to be definitively removed from the social world of the living. However, modern mortality patterns, which put social death ahead of biological death, require us to reconsider this analysis. There is now a premortem liminality. Sometimes it starts at a precise moment in time, as when a person hears a terminal diagnosis or suffers a near-fatal blow from which recovery is unlikely. In other cases the liminal state begins at some indeterminate point when physical and/or mental decline tip the balance between being fully alive and in the process of dying. A classic example is the gradual development of liminality that accompanies chronic conditions such as Alzheimer's disease, in which engagement in the world diminishes slowly over time. At some often disputed point family and friends sense that the person they once knew is no longer there, even if the physical form remains.

A sudden-onset premortem liminality is often experienced as an odd feeling of being a spectator in a world that seems unfazed by a death prediction that changes everything for the subject. I had this sensation when my doctor conveyed a melanoma diagnosis, then coolly rattled off the five-year survival statistics. I felt a rupture in my taken-for-granted world but was startled to find that everyone else seemed to be carrying on as usual. The delusion of self-importance that protects us from having to admit our insignificance is shattered by the realization that our death may be closer than we expected and that this isn't exactly headline news. (Let me hasten to add that my liminal experience was brief, thanks to some quick surgery and annual surveillance.)

Gradual-onset premortem liminality creates complications in a social world that depends on a degree of stability and predictability in human relations. A person afflicted with a progressive disease requires us to continually adjust our expectations of social interaction as new limitations and deficits appear. This is expertly described by Columbia University anthropologist Robert

Murphy in *The Body Silent* (1987), which documents the discomfort of friends and family who were forced to adapt to the author's changing social identity as a spinal cord tumor left him ever more paralyzed. Murphy reflects on the increasingly awkward interactions with friends as he advances to a state of quadriplegia, noting that his identity is progressively "spoiled" by his physical restrictions and by the closeness to death they portend. Despite the fact that his mind is unaffected, there comes a point when he is all but declared dead by everyone save closest relations. He is uncomfortably betwixt and between, too close to biological death to postpone social death any longer.

Whether sudden or gradual, the premortem liminality of social death brings with it some of the same conditions of other liminal states. The person is often secluded, either in a medical institution or in a home transformed by the requirements of nursing care, and limitations on behavior (e.g., mobility, eating, bathing) underscore his/her in-between status just as they do for neophytes in many passage rites. Time can seem frozen or redefined as a futureless present. Status differences evaporate among those who share the liminal condition, as Murphy noticed when hospital staff treated patients without concern for distinctions of gender, age, education, or ethnicity. This leveling of identity markers was especially striking for someone trained to pay attention to the structures of social relations.

Liminal periods in passage rites typically include an educational component, when the subject undergoing transition is instructed about the role he/she is about to occupy. Think of the classes that lead up to Christian confirmation, Jewish bar and bat mitzvahs, or the pastoral counseling that precedes marriage. The liminality of contemporary social death has its own instructional dimension as well, represented in the volumes of self-help books and death-related websites, counseling sessions with religious figures and psychologists, and appointments with medical specialists. There is a push-pull in the messages conveyed by these sources of instruction. On the one hand, there are prescriptions for better dying that set out tasks to accomplish and stages to pass through on the way to a "good death."[2] There are step-by-step accounts of what one can expect as biological death approaches and even how-to manuals for arranging your own departure. Your local funeral home will be glad to assist you in preplanning your "final arrangements." All of this constitutes forward-looking instruction, designed to promote full understanding of an impending biological death.

On the other hand, a vast medical effort is directed at discouraging the person from accepting or even acknowledging that biological death is the natural end point of the transition. Far from facilitating the passage, doctors routinely treat the possibility of death as an avoidable, or at least deferrable, reality, even after the point when their patient's quality of life has so deteriorated as to make mortality the preferable option. They attempt to replace the premortem liminality of social death with another form of liminality: a depersonalized patient tethered to medical instruments and subject to instructions inscribed on a chart. This is the in-between space that Edson's Vivian Bearing occupied.

It's difficult for a person to experience the in-between condition of premortem social death when some cultural experts are pushing forward and others are holding back. I think the mixed message of modern social death—*prepare to die and struggle to live*—is a major source of the contemporary angst about dying and not the often-cited invisibility and loneliness of a medically managed biological death. Liminality is tough to take when the direction of the impending transition is a matter of cultural contention.

Nowhere is the tension between these cultural directives more in evidence than in the relentless conflicts over the issues of physician-assisted death and the treatment of persons diagnosed as being in a persistent vegetative state. In the normal course of medical practice each of these issues is confronted and addressed through the ordinary course of physician-patient-family interaction, but they can also break into public arenas when differences of opinion are resistant to resolution. Sometimes the resulting conflicts become matters of legal and legislative entanglements, with nationwide media attention following every twist and turn. In the next two chapters I consider what we can learn from these conflicts and what they indicate about how the mixed messages of modern social death are being negotiated. In Chapter 4 I tackle the related complication of how and when a person has actually died—how dead is dead enough when medical technology is capable of maintaining the signs of biological functioning?

Complications of Mourning

It is not just the lead-up to death that has become complicated in modern America; the scripts for processing death after-the-fact are also under revision. Many communities within the complex web of American society continue to honor long-held traditions of mourning, with all the attendant rituals. But there have been two significant and interrelated shifts in how deaths are socially and emotionally managed that are affecting all social groups. First, the time frame for mourning has been shortened due to the exigencies of employment obligations for dual-wage-earning families. Federal employees, for example, are limited to thirteen days of sick leave per year for "arrangements necessitated by the death of a family member or [to] attend the funeral of a family member" (USOPM n.d.).[3] Private employers offer varying leave periods for bereavement, but three to five days is standard, depending on how close the relationship of the employee was to the deceased. In the past, women, who bore the brunt of mourning rituals, were not subject to employment-related limits, as most worked only in the home. Today, when it comes to mourning, men and women are on the clock.

The second widespread shift in the societal response to death concerns the increasing medical management of grief. Evolving distinctions are being drawn between the normal and expected period of sorrow at the loss of a loved one and the pathological prolongation of grief behavior that requires medical attention and, often, pharmaceutical intervention. The most recent revision to the American Psychiatric Association's *Diagnostic and Statistical Manual of Mental Disorder* (5th edition, 2013) occasioned much debate about whether grief should ever be considered a mental disorder and, if so, under what conditions. The significance of this debate extends well beyond the confines of medical offices; it has powerful repercussions for the expectations we carry for ourselves and others in the wake of death.

Chapter 5 explores both of these complications in the culture of mourning in contemporary America. I provide some historical and cross-cultural perspective to clarify what it means to abbreviate and medicalize mourning. I ask whether there is significant resistance to these trends and, if so, from what quarters of American society. I argue here, as elsewhere in the book, that the baby-boom demographic is insisting on its own approach to mourning and that they may challenge formulaic approaches to the experience of loss.

To Remember or Forget?

The problem areas surrounding modern mortality extend beyond the process of dying and the immediate emotional aftermath of death. We also face contests over how to dispose of the dead, over what sort of remembrance they are due, and about relations' long-term claims over the remains of their kin. Much to the consternation of funeral home directors, cremation and eco-friendly internments are replacing the more lucrative embalming and coffin business. Remembering the dead with a simple gravestone inscription and obituary may now extend to Facebook posts, car decals, and virtual memorials. Human remains once thought to be of sufficient antiquity to be open to collection and scientific study are now subject to legal claims of ownership from descendants many generations removed from the deceased.

Arguments over how we dispose of and remember the dead reveal a great deal about the contested terrain of death in America, but even more importantly they call our attention to shifting ideas about the physicality of identity. On the one hand, adopting disposal practices that effectively obliterate the physical body rather than preserve it with chemicals that temporarily mask the processes of decomposition indicates a willingness to separate the person from its corporeal container. On the other hand, when Native American groups demand repatriation of bones that are hundreds or, in rare cases, thousands of years old, a continuing connection is being affirmed between not just the original person and his/her bones but also that individual and descendants many times removed. I consider, in Chapter 6, the question "Who owns the bones?" and, in Chapter 7, the problem of remembering the dead.

The Crystal Ball

Reviewing the conflicts that swirl around modern mortality can sometimes feel like déjà vu, with characters changing but the plot remaining pretty much the same. This is especially clear in the public discussions of persistent vegetative states and physician-assisted death. Without paying close attention to the details, it can seem as though America is in a series of looping arguments, not coming closer to any resolution of these serious disputes. By resolution, I do not mean consensus—that is unlikely given the extraordinary diversity of death beliefs found among Americans—but rather a negotiated truce that grants greater tolerance for deeply held convictions on all sides of contentious debates.

I end the book with a close look at whether, nearly two decades into the twenty-first century, we are making any progress on new cultural scripts for dying and death. I have suggested in this introduction that shifting mortality patterns and a reversal of the order of biological and social death have called into question some traditional understandings of the dying process. I have pointed to other stress points in modern mortality, concerning the management of grief and claims on the dead. I conclude with a deceptively simple question: Are we any closer to reaching agreement on how to deal with trouble spots in dying and death than we were when traditional models first began to crumble? What is the future of dying, death, and remembering in America?

Chapter 2

Deciding to Die

My Right to Death with Dignity at 29, by Brittany Maynard

When my suffering becomes too great, I can say to all those I love, "I love you; come be by my side, and come say goodbye as I pass into whatever's next." I will die upstairs in my bedroom with my husband, mother, stepfather and best friend by my side and pass peacefully. I can't imagine trying to rob anyone else of that choice. (Maynard 2014)

Opinion 2.211—Physician-Assisted Suicide

It is understandable, though tragic, that some patients in extreme duress—such as those suffering from a terminal, painful, debilitating illness—may come to decide that death is preferable to life. However, allowing physicians to participate in assisted suicide would cause more harm than good. Physician-assisted suicide is fundamentally incompatible with the physician's role as healer, would be difficult or impossible to control, and would pose serious societal risks. (American Medical Association 1994)

The so-called right-to-die movement in the United States has come a long way. It's original public face was the headline-seeking, combative, and, to many, slightly creepy Dr. Jack Kevorkian, aka Dr. Death, whose "suicide machines" helped dozens of terminally ill persons end their lives before his 1999 arrest, conviction, and imprisonment in Michigan for second-degree murder and illegal

Mortal Dilemmas: The Troubled Landscape of Death in America, by Donald Joralemon, 27–37. © 2016 Left Coast Press, Inc. All rights reserved.

delivery of a controlled substance. During the same period Derek Humphry's best-selling *Final Exit: The Practicalities of Self-Deliverance and Assisted Suicide for the Dying* (1991) and his organization, the Hemlock Society, grabbed the public's attention with how-to advice on life-ending techniques. At the same time, advocates for "death with dignity" were promoting legislation to permit physicians to assist in the intentional death of terminally ill persons who requested help. The first such law in the United States was Oregon's Death with Dignity Act (1997); Washington (2008), Vermont (2013) and California (2015) followed suit, and Montana's supreme court (2009) removed legal impediments to doctors assisting patients to fulfill their wish to die.[1] On the other side of the issue, over thirty states passed laws criminalizing physician-assisted death, and related public referenda failed in multiple states.

Two separate advocacy groups merged in 2005 to form Compassion and Choices, the largest and most active advocacy group supporting right-to-die legislation. It adopted a sophisticated approach to public relations, for example, by insisting on replacing "assisted suicide" with "aid in dying" and focusing its rhetoric on the very American themes of choice and control. The organization gave a public platform to Brittany Maynard, the Californian who was forced to relocate to Oregon to end her suffering from a particularly aggressive and terminal brain cancer under that state's Death with Dignity legislation (see Figure 2.1). Maynard was frustrated and resentful that, on top of having to deal with the devastating effects of her illness, she had to move her family just to be allowed the right to orchestrate her own death so that it could be peaceful and free of the pain that the tumor would have otherwise inflicted. She did not want to have the last hours or days of her life spent in a state of complete sedation, but neither did she judge those who make that choice. She wanted to control the manner of her own death. Somewhat cautiously, given the precarious condition of her health, she agreed to tell her story in two videos and through a series of high-profile interviews because she wanted to bring attention to the real impact of laws prohibiting physicians from assisting in a terminal patient's death (Daniel Diaz, personal communication). In Maynard, Compassion and Choices had a far more compelling and attractive spokesperson than the eccentric Dr. Death.

The principal opposition to physician-assisted death comes from the Catholic Church and some Protestant evangelical organizations, national hospice organizations, and disability rights advocates. Although the American Medical Association adopted a position against the practice (see above quote), polls show that increasing numbers of doctors support a medical role in ending the life of a person in the later stages of a terminal illness if protections against coercion

Figure 2.1   Brittany Maynard.
Photograph courtesy of Daniel Diaz and the BrittanyFund.org.

are included. Until recently general public polling indicated a nearly even split between opponents and proponents, with some significant differences on the basis of race, ethnicity, and religion: a majority of white mainline Protestants supported laws allowing doctors to aid death decisions, whereas African American Protestants, white evangelical Protestants, and Hispanic Catholics disapproved by a margin of two-to-one (Pew Research Center 2013a).[2] However, in the aftermath of publicity generated by Brittany Maynard's story, a Health Day/Harris poll revealed a significant shift in favor of a physician assisting in a terminal patient's request for medical treatment to end their own life, with 72 percent of respondents approving (Harris Polls 2014).

In the following discussion I use the concepts introduced in Chapter 1 to set the debate about physician-assisted death (PAD) in the wider context of epidemiological, medical, and demographic realities. Then I review the main arguments for and against PAD in the United States with an eye to the cultural underpinnings of the positions. I argue that this very contentious issue, like all those this book reviews, is socially and culturally problematic because it tracks along fundamental divides between competing ethical principals and cultural assumptions. I end with my own take on where the argument is headed.

Context for the Debate

First, a word about terminology. I choose to use the expression *physician-assisted death* (PAD) rather than any of the alternative versions because it is important that an analysis of the debate not privilege either side. The negative associations with the word *suicide*—that it is a senseless death and evidence of mental illness—prejudges what is exactly at the core of the argument between opponents and proponents, namely whether persons suffering from a terminal illness can be making a rational and sane choice when they decide to end their lives. By the same token, the expressions *death with dignity* or *aid in dying* are equally prejudicial in that they convey a positive interpretation that opponents reject. No term is ideal, but PAD at least offers a middle ground between linguistic options that favor one or the other side of the dispute.

The emergence of a debate about PAD is linked to the epidemiological and medical developments discussed in Chapter 1. The expanding capacity of biomedicine to treat the infectious diseases that were once responsible for the majority of deaths in America led to greater longevity and to an increasing percentage of mortality statistics linked to chronic conditions like cancer, heart disease, and degenerative neurological conditions. Furthermore, even those chronic conditions came to be targets of medical interventions that often delay a fatal outcome. For example, cancers that would otherwise threaten survival in the short term are slowed or even reversed by combinations of sophisticated surgeries, new pharmaceuticals, radiation treatments, and chemotherapies. The evolution of emergency and intensive-care technologies have also played a role in creating a population surviving with conditions that would have otherwise resulted in speedy deaths, including those that trigger PAD discussions.

Not only are more people living longer due to improved medical care, with each passing year there are also larger percentages of persons over the age of sixty-five due to the post–World War II demographic explosion known as the

Baby Boom Generation and to birthrates that have dropped precipitously since the early 1970s. Over 14 percent of Americans in 2015 were over sixty-five, compared to just 4 percent in 1900, and that is expected to grow to over 19 percent (72 million) by 2030. The consequences of the graying of America are many, but one significant factor is that larger numbers of people will have the experience of caring for persons in compromised health conditions and/ or having direct personal experience with deteriorating health. Public opinion polls like the Pew study cited above show that approval of life-ending actions in late stages of terminal illnesses increases with the age of the respondents.

An additional contextual factor is the increasing percentage of deaths that occur in medical settings under the management of doctors. This effectively puts the physician in a central role in most end-of-life decisions, a responsibility that many patients and family members are glad to relinquish to the experts. Because the medical imperative is to continue treating even in the face of di- minishing returns—when suffering increases with little or no real benefit to the patient—yielding power to doctors can and often does mean that terminally ill patients are confused and desperate, torn between the false promise of relief and catastrophic decline.[3] Until recently and, in many American hospitals, still, inadequate attention has been paid to the relief of pain. The option of hospice care, including palliative medication, is typically introduced to patients and families far too late to take advantage of the multifaceted care giving that those institutions can provide. We have to be honest about the fact that these shortcomings in the medical management of terminal illnesses are part of the backdrop to the debate about PAD.

Beyond medical and demographic factors, the debate about PAD in the United States is also shaped by the fact that other developed countries permit even more medical involvement in life-ending decisions than in Oregon, Washington, Vermont, and California. Proponents of PAD frequently cite permissive laws in the Netherlands and Switzerland to suggest that the United States is behind the curve.[4] The Swiss organization Dignitas (www.dignitas.ch) even provides death services to citizens of countries where PAD is illegal. The World Federation of Right to Die Societies (www.worldrtd.net) counts twenty-three countries as members and engages in international advocacy work to promote PAD. This international context must also be considered as we review the course of argu- ments in the United States.

In summary, debates about PAD in America should be seen in light of the fact that more people are experiencing, directly or indirectly, the sorts of ter- minal illnesses that initiate consideration of PAD and that, although the public as a whole has been divided on the idea, an aging cohort is more positively inclined to agree that ending one's life is a moral and reasonable action in the face of terminal illness. Faults in the medical management of dying in America and international advocacy for PAD also set the stage for spirited battles in the courts, voting booths, and state legislatures. Now it's time to turn to the positions staked out by both sides, using the concise review written for the Hastings Center by Timothy Quill and Jane Greenlaw (2008) as a point of departure.

Arguments in Favor of PAD

The central pillar in the case for PAD is the principle of personal autonomy, the idea that individuals should be able to act according to their own wishes and free of coercion from others. Autonomy figures prominently in the most widely adopted framework in bioethics and is tied to the influential moral theory of the German philosopher Immanuel Kant. The principle played a central role in developing the Patient Self-Determination Act (1990), which set the standard for informed-consent regulations in all health care settings. It has been invoked to justify a patient's choice to decline or request withdrawal of treatment. In essence, proponents of PAD argue that an individual's right to make medical choices for him/herself should extend to the decision to end his/her life rather than endure the extreme suffering that often accompanies the final stage of terminal diseases.[5]

The application of the principle of autonomy in medicine can be traced to the patients' rights movement of the 1970s, which came in part as a response to the paternalism that had long framed the relationship between doctor and patient—"Doctor knows best"—and to the accumulating evidence of racial and gender discrimination in medical research and clinical care. It was seen as a necessary corrective to patients being subject to treatments and research protocols they neither understood nor desired. The self-directed person that autonomy promotes resonates with the individualism that is a common thread in American political thought and social life. Tying PAD to this culturally appealing view is a powerful strategy.

The other two lines of argument in favor of PAD speak to the responsibilities of physicians to terminally ill patients. First, it is the doctor's obligation to act mercifully when a patient is experiencing such extreme pain that no medication is effective in providing relief. The priority to relieve that suffering trumps all other considerations, even if hastening death is a consequence. Second, it is unacceptable for a physician to abandon the patient in such a condition; being present through the dying process is a requirement of proper care. Each of these declarations emerge from another core principle in bioethics, the notion of beneficence, the ethic that physicians should always act to benefit their patients. Again, linking PAD to such an appealing notion adds emotional weight to the positive argument.

It is important to note that the case for PAD is contingent on the concept of suffering, frequently interpreted in the reductionist terms of physical pain. We will see that opponents reject the idea that intractable and severe pain can ever serve as a justification for life-ending actions, but at this point I want to note that suffering can extend well beyond the physical experience of pain. Persons contemplating PAD likely have more on their minds than just ending the experience of pain, and both proponents and opponents should address a more inclusive definition of suffering.

Arguments Against PAD

The opposition to PAD fundamentally comes down to the conviction that nothing justifies taking a life or assisting in someone else's suicide—and this is the term opponents prefer. Religiously inspired versions of this core belief, based on the sanctity-of-life philosophy, assert that only God should determine when and how we die. Variations that come from medical sources insist that doctors must be committed "to do no harm" (the principle of nonmaleficence in Kantian terms), a prime directive that prohibits physicians from assisting in a patient's death. So-called full palliation, in which pain medications are dosed to leave the patient effectively unconscious, is presented as the ethical alternative to treating end-stage suffering. Hospice philosophy is centered on the notion that the "natural" course of dying should be permitted, with pain medication used to diminish and control suffering.

An important second line of criticism relates to what opponents fear will result should PAD be normalized, the "slippery slope" of accepting assisted death. Hospice advocates are threatened by the possibility that the end-of-life care they offer will lose in a competition with an option that offers a quicker and painless death. They urge improvements and expansion of hospice services as well as better public education campaigns to overcome misperceptions about hospice rather than a legalized PAD. They envision a spiral of PAD cases as the public becomes accustomed to the idea and as health insurers recognize the cost savings entailed by faster deaths.

Perhaps the most compelling version of the slippery slope argument comes from the disability rights community.[6] Those with serious disabilities and the family members who care for them fear that an inevitable expansion of criteria for PAD-eligible patients will come to include anyone whose care costs too much or whose life value is called into question. For good historical reasons, they feel vulnerable to any public policy that might be used to distinguish those who are and are not worthy of being kept alive. This fear is expressed not only in the arguments about PAD but also in the discussion of persons in persistent vegetative states, as we will see in the next chapter.

Rebuttals and Predictions

Two lines of argument have been the focus of attention in the back-and-forth between proponents and opponents. The first is whether PAD constitutes killing and is therefore both morally wrong and a violation of medical ethics. Advocates of PAD argue that it is the disease that is killing the person and that the lethal drug made available by a physician under legal guidelines merely provides a measure of control over the time and circumstances of death. They also claim that there is a thin line between PAD and the legally recognized right of patients to refuse treatment or demand the withdrawal of life-sustaining interventions, so called passive euthanasia. Both involve a medical orchestration of a terminal disease's final stage; they differ only by how long the person is made to suffer before death.

Critics reject the claim that PAD is anything but medical murder and insist that there is a meaningful difference between stopping treatment and providing lethal drugs. They claim that good pain control is available to minimize suffering and that only an ill-informed and desperate person would contemplate suicide. They also point to the risk of persons being coerced, explicitly or by subtle pressure, into ending their lives so as not to be a further burden on their families.

The slippery slope argument has also generated rebuttals. Proponents draw on statistics from Oregon to show that the number of persons taking advantage of that state's PAD statute is small and stable, accounting for one in a thousand deaths for the first ten years that the law was in effect. There is also evidence that more people go through the process to acquire the lethal drug than actually end up using it. Similar low rates have been documented in the Netherlands, where PAD has been permitted for thirty years (Quill and Greenlaw 2008).[7] Advocates point to this evidence to refute the idea that allowing PAD will inevitably result in its expansion to persons whose medical situation was not envisioned by the original law or to those whose disabilities might make them vulnerable to abuse under the pretext of assisting death. In the proponent's view there is no slippery slope and the risk of coercion is overstated.

The other side notes that the legal use of PAD is still in its early stages and that evidence from just one state is hardly sufficient to calm fears of misuse. Critics see the evidence from the Netherlands as confirmation of their predictions, as PAD is performed in that country even in circumstances when the person has not requested it, when they are in extreme pain from a terminal illness and have lost the ability to communicate their desires. Although these cases represent a very small percentage of PADs—less than 1 percent—opponents take them as proof that giving physicians the power to end lives comes with unacceptable risks.

To this point advocates for PAD note that American doctors are often complicit in the deaths of patients who are critically ill and unable to communicate, typically with the consent of family and/or by following prior instructions in the form of a living will from the person. They ask how a do not resuscitate (DNR) order that stops life-saving interventions is different from administering a life-ending medication. How is removing breathing and heart-assist technology from a patient with end-stage coronary artery disease, knowing that the result will be death, any less "killing" than what critics see in PAD? Is PAD really different, beyond duration, from applying pain medication at levels known to be fatal?

Ethicists attempt to distinguish these acts from PAD with the term *passive euthanasia* and with the so-called doctrine of double effect. Passive euthanasia refers to a physician's action or inaction that hastens a patient's death. The doctrine of double effect applies when the intention of that doctor is to relieve suffering, not to end a life. In the above cases the doctor's actions would be considered ethical under this doctrine so long as his/her intention was to care, not kill. I come back to this argument in the next chapter, but here I would join those who insist that this is a distinction without a difference. A doctor who turns off a breathing machine or steps up intravenous pain medication to life-threatening levels knows perfectly well that he/she is hastening death and in most cases is doing so precisely because either the patient or family members have indicated that this is their wish. As a personal matter, I don't see how PAD can earn the charge of killing while these actions are considered ethical. Neither deserves the label, in my view.

Comments and Predictions

The debate about PAD should sound familiar. On the one hand, it invokes the powerful American values of self-determination, choice, liberty, and privacy.

On the other, it summons the equally central ideas of the inherent value of life, of familial and medical care-giving responsibilities, and of the notion of God's will. These values and some of the same constituencies supporting them have been at the heart of other medically related debates in America, most notably over a woman's right to abortion, and we will see them reemerge in the next chapter in regard to the treatment of persons diagnosed as being in a persistent vegetative state.

One perplexing part of the debate about PAD is the use of the phrase *natural course of the disease*. It appears in the care philosophy of hospice as the standard it aims to achieve—namely to let persons proceed to death by the "natural" impact of the disease on their bodies, with only pain medication and excellent nursing care as interventions. It is also invoked by religious figures who demand that nothing replace God's will as a person nears the end of life. But what is "natural" about a disease process that has in virtually every case been subject to all manner of medical treatment, some so toxic that they are nearly as dangerous as the underlying condition? The body that makes it to hospice has already been subject to everything from extreme surgeries to devastating chemotherapies. To argue that it is possible to allow the disease to "take its course" after applying the full force of contemporary medical science seems naïve. Hasn't that horse already left the barn?

Looking forward, it seems likely to me that efforts to legalize PAD will continue to move forward on a state-by-state basis. Older Americans will constitute ever-larger percentages of the voting public, and research suggests that they favor PAD at levels significantly greater than the public as a whole. Unless data from those states in which PAD is legal shifts toward the doomsday scenario painted by opponents, the force of experience will add weight to the case in favor of legalization. There will continue to be very public cases, like Brittany Maynard, that generate sympathy for those who make the decision to end their lives. Finally, I see nothing to indicate that medicine will step back from the clinical practices that inflict harm in the name of vanishing hope to those nearing the end of a terminal illness. This alone will continue to drive interest in an alternative pathway to death, one that permits a degree of control and the promise of a painless departure. I return to this vision of our medical future in my concluding chapter.

There will, in my estimation, remain powerful segments of American society who will resist the expansion of PAD and will never become a part of the population that seeks it for themselves or their family members. Just as abortion remains a divisive topic in America because it draws compelling core values into conflict with one another, so will PAD continue to spark vehement protests between persons and groups laying claim to central principles that are at odds when applied to this debate. Unless the US Supreme Court reverses previous rulings related to PAD and decides there is a constitutional basis for a right to assistance in dying or future federal legislation prohibits it—neither of which is likely, in my view—the result will be that the map of America will include a majority of states that allow PAD and a minority that do not.

PAD is and will remain a trouble spot in America's management of dying, but an even more problematic issue concerns how we treat persons who have suffered such a catastrophic loss of biological function that they are without the capacity to communicate or, arguably, to even engage in the world but are not yet medically "dead." I refer to the controversial diagnosis of persistent vegetative states. This is the next of America's mortal dilemmas for us to consider.

Chapter 3

Liminal People, Hard Decisions

The claimed interests of the State in this case are essentially the preservation and sanctity of human life and defense of the right of the physician to administer medical treatment according to his best judgment. . . . We think that the State's interest contra weakens and the individual's right to privacy grows as the degree of bodily invasion increases and the prognosis dims. Ultimately there comes a point at which the individual's rights overcome the State interest. (*In Re Quinlan*, 70 N.J. 10, 355 A.2d 647 (1976), 24)

We in government have a duty to protect the weak, disabled and vulnerable. I appreciate the efforts of state and federal lawmakers on both sides of the aisle who have taken this duty to heart. (Governor John Ellis "Jeb" Bush, in Vries 2005)

There may be as many as thirty-five thousand Americans diagnosed as being in a vegetative state (VS), and nearly 30 percent of them are children.[1] This "disorder of consciousness," which also goes by the name unresponsive wakefulness syndrome results from severe brain damage that leaves the person without any awareness of self or surroundings, although reflexive behavior and sleep-wake cycles are preserved. These later characteristics distinguish the condition from a coma, which is a state of extreme unresponsiveness that may even resist arousal by painful stimuli.[2] Some undetermined percentage of VS patients may instead be in a minimally conscious state, a more recent diagnosis meant to capture those patients who show some evidence of consciousness, such as the ability to

Mortal Dilemmas: The Troubled Landscape of Death in America, by Donald Joralemon, 39–58. © 2016 Left Coast Press, Inc. All rights reserved.

follow commands and display purposeful behavior, at least on an intermittent basis. The prognosis for VS patients is poor and more certain as time progresses.

The most common cause of a VS is blunt-force trauma to the brain, most often in car accidents or as a result of a gunshot wound to the head, but anything that interrupts blood flow to the brain for more than four minutes can also cause sufficient neural damage to leave the person in this condition. This later category of causes would include heart attack, near drowning, suffocation, and drug overdose. Rounding out the causes of a VS are a variety of degenerative and metabolic disorders (e.g., Alzheimer's disease, mitochondrial encephalopathy) and developmental malformations (e.g., anencephaly).

Patients in a VS require constant nursing attention and artificial nutrition and hydration (ANH), but so long as the neural damage does not extend to the brain stem, they are often able to breathe without mechanical assistance and their nervous system continues to maintain body temperature. The cost of lifetime care for VS patients ranges from $600,000 to $1,875,000 (Giacino et al. 2002). Most will live out their days in nursing homes, but a sizeable proportion of VS children are cared for at home. It is very common for family members to sign do not resuscitate (DNR) orders for VS patients and for authorized family members to give medical instructions that prohibit the use of antibiotics to treat infections such as pneumonia (Jennett 2002).

Some of the most public controversies related to dying in America stem from the wrenching decisions that physicians and family members have to make for VS patients as time progresses and prognosis dims. Specifically, is it ethical to end the ANH that is alternatively presented as a life-prolonging medical treatment or ordinary and morally required care? Is there a difference between withholding antibiotics to treat infections that have the potential to end a VS patient's life and withdrawing food and water to accomplish the same end? Who is entitled to make that decision, substituting his/her judgment for the person who can no longer communicate? These are the questions we need to consider in the context of cultural priorities and legal/historical context.

Contexts

As in the discussion of physician-assisted death, we have to begin with a terminological clarification. The medical literature on this topic frequently distinguishes between persistent and permanent vegetative states, where the first would be diagnosed after a month from the original traumatic or non-traumatic brain injury and in the absence of improvement. Applying the term *permanent,* by contrast, is a prognosis based on a physician's probabilistic esti-mation that the condition is irreversible. This judgment is based on the length of time the condition has lasted, the history of diagnostic tests on the patient, and wider clinical experience with long-lasting vegetative states. Because the term *permanent* carries with it significant implications for the decisions family members have to make and because it can be taken by interested parties to involve degrees of uncertainty, I choose to defer using the distinction by refer-ring to vegetative states (VS) without additional qualifiers until the question of reversibility figures prominently in the analysis.

Disputes over the withdrawal of life support from severely incapacitated individuals arise, in part, from the fully understandable emotions that ac-company the dying of a relative or close friend. If humans found it easy to release kin to death, there would be no need for the kinds of rituals that even the earliest Homo sapiens practiced when someone died. However, factors peculiar to America during the past three decades further complicate the living's response to the dying and have set the stage for widely publicized conflicts over the sorts of death decisions that arise in VS cases. Before con-sidering these cases in detail it is important to explore the context within which they developed.

In Chapter 1 I argued that twentieth-century medical innovations in devel-oped countries created the conditions for a reversal of biological and social death, with chronic illnesses and longer life spans resulting in people undergoing a premortem social death before a delayed biological death. The discussion of physician-assisted death reviewed in the last chapter emerged in large measure as a consequence of this development because modern medicine prolongs the period of suffering from chronic illnesses with a terminal prognosis to the point that ending life becomes, for some, the preferable option. Effectively PAD is the declaration by a sufferer that social death is complete and biological death should proceed. We saw that the issues of autonomy and the sanctity of human life were prominent in the PAD debate.

The circumstances surrounding VS are both similar to and, in significant ways, different from those we encountered in regard to PAD. They are similar in that medicine in both cases is often responsible for the continuation of bio-logical life beyond the point many consider a meaningful social life. As we'll see in the following cases, emergency medicine and intensive care preserved biological functioning and delayed the biological deaths that would otherwise have transpired. This leaves behind "liminal persons," neither dead nor fully living. Like PAD cases, the question for VS patients often comes down to the balance between life as a value unto itself and death as a release from suffering.

The critical difference between PAD and VS patients is that by legal definition in the states that permit assisted death the person is conscious and capable of making an autonomous decision, to exercise the right of self-determination. For the majority of VS patients the suddenness and severity of the trauma that destroyed brain function left no opportunity to convey personal wishes unless the individual had communicated his/her preferences beforehand in a fashion acceptable to physicians and/or the courts (e.g., an unambiguous and legally recognized living will). This means that the question of autonomy is complicated by often contested claims of surrogate decision makers, typically close family members who insist they know what the VS patient would have wanted had they been able to communicate.

The fact that a surrogate is most often responsible for care decisions is, I think, the reason that direct life-ending measures like those involved in PAD are rarely debated in VS cases. Intentionally ending your own life to avoid suffering is one thing; allowing someone else to make that decision for you when you are unable to communicate is quite another, at least if we are to credit public surveys (Pew Research Center 2013b). For VS patients, life-ending decisions involve withdrawing or withholding treatment, with the most contentious being the removal of the feeding tube that provides ANH directly into the stomach through an abdominal incision after a procedure called percutaneous endoscopic gastrostomy (PEG). Not only is the ethical status of withdrawing life-prolonging treatments questioned—an issue I raised in the last chapter—but also disputed is whether ANH should even be considered a medical treatment rather than ordinary care like that provided by nurses. We'll see that the symbolic value of food and water comes into play in the debate.

The right of a surrogate to make a decision to withdraw ANH as well as the medical status of that intervention has been central to legal cases brought as a result of VS disputes. By 1990 there had already been twenty-six suits in American courts over this issue (Weir and Gostin 1990); the cases reviewed below were the most widely reported. The right of a conscious person to refuse medical treatment has been consistently affirmed in these legal proceedings. They have considered what requirements for surrogate decisions apply when the person is unable to communicate and has left only hearsay evidence regarding his/her preferences. Courts have also weighed in on whether ANH should be treated in the same way as other medical interventions. We will come back to this point as we analyze the three most famous VS legal suits.

There are even more complicated philosophical and spiritual questions raised by VS patients. A task force asked to review medical aspects of the vegetative state declared: "By definition, patients in a persistent vegetative state are unaware of themselves or their environment. They are noncognitive, nonsentient, and incapable of conscious experience" (Multi-Society Task Force 1994). Does that mean that they are no longer "persons" in the ordinary sense of the word? If so, does a different standard of care apply? Are we obligated to preserve biological functioning when the patient has irreversibly lost the defining characteristics of personhood? And is there a risk, as disability rights advocates insist, that the same argument will be made for severely disabled persons who are not in a VS but who lack some or all of the same capacities?

These questions should remind us of the debates about abortion in the United States. Here, too, passionate disagreements about the minimal conditions for personhood divide sectors of American society and influence the course of judicial decisions. It isn't surprising, given the parallel issues involved, that many of the same groups that advocate for broader definitions of personhood during gestation are also vocal in the discussions about the rights of persons at the end of life. Assertions of the sanctity of life are applied to fetuses and VS patients alike and for some of the same moral reasons.

Debates about VS may have been precipitated by developments in medicine, but they are taking place in a heterogeneous nation where multiple parties contend for the right to be heard on matters of values and ethics. Particularly significant for these life-cycle issues has been the reemergence in the late twentieth century of conservative religious groups acting as a potent political force. Conservative Protestant evangelicals and Catholic charismatics[3] promote an approach to American civic life that challenges the historical division between church and state in favor of a public policy in line with Christian dogma, as interpreted by leaders who take biblical teaching literally and/or adhere strictly to papal instruction. They are united in their opposition to abortion, their support for a variety of religiously inspired educational reforms (e.g., the teaching of creationism or "intelligent design" in the public schools, prayer in the classroom, "abstinence only" instruction for sexual education, public financing for religious affiliated schools) and in a rigid rejection of medical interventions that hasten death. They also share an antipathy to judicial decisions that find a constitutional foundation for the separation of church and state, a right of privacy that extends to life-and-death medical decisions, and a balance of powers between executive, judicial, and legislative branches of government.

This is certainly not the first time in American history that religious groups have gained sufficient political power to influence public policy, sometimes in conservative directions (e.g., the temperance movement) and at other times toward more liberal objectives (e.g., abolition and the civil rights movement). What is novel about the current situation is the speed with which Christian evangelicals have been able to mobilize when called upon to support or oppose pending legislative actions or court decisions. Facilitated by the organization of megachurches, broadcast ministries (radio and television), sympathetic media, and the resources of the Internet, evangelical leaders have little difficulty producing tidal waves of e-mails and phone calls to political representatives or in turning out large and vocal street protests. This will be evident as we recall the torturous history of the three most famous VS patients.

From Karen to Terri

Three women, united by the tragic circumstances of their deaths, are icons of contentious dying in the public mind: Karen Ann Quinlan, Nancy Cruzan, and Theresa (Terri) Marie Schiavo. Each suffered severe trauma to the brain, was resuscitated and put on life-support equipment, eventually received a diagnosis of persistent or permanent vegetative state, and became the focus of high-profile court proceedings when one or more family member requested that life support measures be withdrawn. It is not, however, the commonalities of the three cases that draw my attention; I find the differences far more instructive for an understanding of shifts in American views of dying and death.

Karen Quinlan and the Respirator

Momentous events competed for headlines in April of 1975. Watergate conspirators had recently been sentenced to long prison terms, President Ford was desperately trying to disengage from Vietnam before Saigon fell, and a civil war that was to last for fifteen years broke out in Lebanon. Initially little notice was taken of a twenty-one-year-old New Jersey woman's plight when she arrived at Newton Memorial Hospital after losing consciousness at a party and suffering two prolonged periods without breathing (for at least fifteen minutes each time, according to court documents). Karen Quinlan was resuscitated, put on a respirator, and subsequently transferred to a Catholic hospital, St. Clare's, in Morris County. By late May physicians had determined she was in a "chronic persistent vegetative state," had no cognitive function, and would never recover.

The lack of public attention was about to change. Quinlan's adoptive parents, with the support of their parish priest, decided that their daughter would not have wished to be kept alive under these conditions. In August they asked doctors to remove Karen's respirator, providing signed documents absolving the hospital and her physicians of liability. The St. Clare's lawyers refused, the case went to court, and the media began to pay attention. Local, national, and even international news outlets gave this "right to die" case extensive coverage.

After losing in a Morris County court, the Quinlans appealed to the New Jersey Supreme Court. The hospital's lawyers, the county prosecutor, and the state attorney general argued, "The Court had no jurisdiction to grant the Quinlan's request, a person's best interest is never served by allowing them to die, there is no constitutional right to die, the State's interest in the preservation of life overrides the guarantees in the First and Eighth Amendments, granting the request would be against prevailing medical standards and ceasing treatment would be homicide if Karen died" ("Legal Implications" 2006).

On March 31, 1976, the decision was issued; the Quinlans won with a unanimous verdict. The court decided that there is a right of privacy protected by the Constitution, that this right is not voided by a person's inability to speak or act for him/herself, that Quinlan's parents were in a good position to judge what Karen would have wanted, and that the state's interest in life diminishes in proportion to the hopelessness of a medical prognosis and the invasiveness of medical interventions (see above quote). Without further appeal, the Quinlan parents ordered the removal of Karen's respirator but left her nasal feeding tube in place. Against all expectations, she was successfully weaned from the respirator and began to breathe on her own. She was moved to a nursing home, where she survived for nearly ten more years, finally dying due to pneumonia-related respiratory failure on June 11, 1985.

There are several points to keep in mind before we move on to the second of the precedent-setting cases. First, despite the fact that it was a Catholic hospital that sought to block the Quinlan's wishes, the public debate about Karen was largely secular and cast in terms of individual autonomy and patient rights. Even Father Trapasso, the Quinlans' priest, commented that he supported their choice in spite of his opposition to euthanasia because "We have a right to decide how we should be treated" (Pfister 2005). Second, the Quinlans asked that Karen be removed from a respirator, but when she started to breathe on her own, they did not follow up with a request for removal of the feeding tube. We'll want to look at what happens when feeding rather than breathing is at issue.

Finally, the Quinlan legal case had as much to do with the assumed authority of physicians as with questions about the withdrawal of life support per se. The physicians at St. Clare were defending what they took to be doctors' rights and responsibilities to make life-and-death decisions about their patients. The traditional role of the doctor as the sole authority for medical decisions had come under attack during the previous decade, when the paternalism of biomedicine was challenged by an activist women's health movement and by severe criticism of unethical behavior in medical research. The Quinlan family's insistence on the right to order doctors to end medical treatment was another skirmish in the battle to prioritize patients over their doctors in the decision-making process.

Nancy Cruzan and the Religious Right

There were many right-to-die trials, many concerning VS patients, in the years following the Quinlan case, as many as fifty-four between 1976 and 1988 across the United States. The next to gain true national prominence began on a Missouri road late at night on January 11, 1983. Nancy Cruzan, a twenty-five-year-old woman driving alone, lost control of her car and was thrown from the vehicle as it rolled. Emergency personnel found her face down in a ditch with no heartbeat; estimates are that she had not been breathing for at least twelve minutes. She was resuscitated and transported to a hospital, where she was eventually given a permanent vegetative state diagnosis. Her husband authorized the use of a feeding tube, but her parents were eventually assigned guardianship when he later agreed to the dissolution of their marriage. When the Cruzans concluded, after three years, that Nancy would never recover, they initiated a legal petition for permission to withdraw "artificial nutrition and hydration" (i.e., the feeding tube) from their daughter. An initial finding in their favor was overturned by the Missouri Supreme Court in a decision that was subsequently sustained on appeal to the US Supreme Court (Cruzan v. Director, Missouri Department of Health, 88-1503, 497 U. S. 261, 1990). This was the first such case to have reached the High Court.

The irony is that the Cruzans and the right-to-die movement in some ways actually won by losing. The Court majority accepted that "a competent person would have a constitutionally protected right to refuse lifesaving hydration and nutrition" and restricted itself to considering the conditions that would have to be met for a surrogate to make the same decision on behalf of an "incompetent person"—that is, someone who is not able to decide for him/herself. It agreed with the lower court that the states have a constitutional right to set the bar high for a decision that will result in the incompetent person's death. The standard of "clear and convincing evidence" used by the Missouri court in rejecting the parents' claim that they knew Nancy would have wanted to die was, in the view of a majority of the justices of the Supreme Court, reasonable in balancing the right to refuse treatment against the state's interests (e.g., preservation of life, protection of persons from abuse by surrogates). In short, the Court provided a firm constitutional foundation for the refusal of medical treatment, including a feeding tube, while giving the individual states latitude in determining what level of evidence would be required of a surrogate as proof of an incompetent person's wishes.

Six months after the Supreme Court ruling the Cruzans returned to the lower court with new evidence that Nancy had expressed in conversations with friends a clear opinion about never wanting to be kept alive in a vegetative state. This time the judge accepted the testimony as "clear and convincing evidence" and granted the Cruzans the right to have Nancy's feeding tube removed. She died on December 26, 1990, twelve days after the tubes were removed and nearly eight years after the car accident that destroyed her brain.

The Cruzan case unfolded just a few years after Karen Quinlan's, but a political shift to the right in the United States, embodied by the 1980 election of Ronald Reagan as president, guaranteed that Nancy's situation would spark a very different public reaction. Conservative evangelicals had been organized as a potent voting block by Jerry Falwell's "Moral Majority" organization (founded in 1979), and their anger at a judiciary seen to be out of step with Christian values was focused on three issues: voluntary prayer in the public schools, abortion, and any form of euthanasia (including the withdrawal of life support). Highly effective means of communication with church congregations around the country and impressive financial resources gave evangelical leaders the tools to mobilize large numbers of supporters to vote for their preferred candidates in local, state, and national contests. These tools also enabled leaders to call for public protests as needed.

Evangelical influence in Missouri is substantial. As much as a third of the state's population identifies as "born again," the headquarters for a number of national Pentecostal and other evangelical organizations are located there (e.g., United Pentecostal Church, Assemblies of God, Association of General Baptists), and conservative evangelicals contributed significantly to Republican wins in Missouri in several presidential elections (e.g., Ronald Reagan in 1980, George W. Bush in 2000 and 2004). John David Ashcroft, a powerful figure in evangelical politics, was the Missouri state attorney general (1976–1984) and then governor (1984–1992) while the Cruzan case made its way to the Supreme Court. The Cruzans' lawyer, William H. Colby, believes that Ashcroft supported the case against the Cruzans. Mr. Ashcroft, the son of an evangelical minister and faithful member of the Assembly of God, eventually became US attorney general in George W. Bush's first term. The religious right considered him their most important friend in the Bush administration.[4]

It should come as no surprise, then, that evangelical protestors arrived at the hospital where Nancy Cruzan lay dying. Randall Terry, founder of the extreme group Operation Rescue, joined his protestors, who held signs reading "Murder or Mercy?" and "Feed Nancy." On December 18 a number of the protestors attempted to enter the facility, claiming that they wanted to reinsert Nancy's feeding tube, and many were arrested. PBS's *Frontline* recorded the views of the protestors for "The Death of Nancy Cruzan," aired on March 24, 1992:

1st PROTESTER: If I could get up there—I know they've got pretty good nurses in there—I would put the tube back in her myself. I had hoped to be able to try something like that, but we're not going to make it.

4th PROTESTER: "Vegetable" is going to be just like fetus was. That's the word they're going to use. It's not fully human and you can kill it. A vegetable isn't human.

6th PROTESTER: I mean, a person can't be a vegetable. They have a soul, they have a heart, there's no way—

4th PROTESTER: America has lost all sense of value for human life at all, you know, with abortion and now with this thing with Nancy.

PROTEST LEADER: Oh, Jesus, mighty power and shake up Satan's kingdom! Shake up Satan's kingdom! Throw a monkey wrench in this business. Bring our nation back to God, Mighty Father. Forgive the people. Professing Christians can be so cold and heartless and stupid. Oh, God, hear our voice and intervene by the fire of the spirit of God! Glory to God! Work a miracle on her behalf and turn our hearts back to—

As Nancy neared death another Operation Rescue associate, the Reverend Patrick J. Mahoney from Boca Raton, Florida, went to the US Court of Appeals for the Eighth Circuit (St. Louis) to ask for a resumption of feeding on the grounds that a former hospital chaplain reportedly had seen Nancy react when told that she was going to die. The court refused the petition because the Reverend Mahoney had no standing in the case ("Cruzan's Condition Downgraded to Critical" 1990). A number of other last-minute appeals met with a similar fate. Even Governor Ashcroft, who initially attempted to force the reinsertion of the feeding tube, eventually gave up.

Despite the evidence of evangelical involvement, it would be a mistake to view the opposition to the Cruzan family as exclusively religious. Evangelical protestors helped to bring press coverage to the struggle, but there was greater public ambivalence about Nancy's situation than in the Quinlan case, precisely because it was a feeding tube and not a mechanical respirator that the family wanted removed. Donald Lamkins, the hospital administrator at the facility where Cruzan was being cared for, voiced this broader concern to *Frontline*:

"We know that we can unplug a machine. That's been talked about in so many places. TV shows have shown that. That isn't nearly [as] hard for us to accept. But the fact that we starve somebody to death—we don't do that. That's—that's beyond our ability to think, even, at this point, in Missouri."

As a legal matter, the justices of the Supreme Court in the Cruzan case determined that there is no meaningful distinction to be drawn between a feeding tube and a respirator. In the majority opinion Chief Justice William Rehnquist wrote, "The court acknowledged the 'emotional significance' of food, but noted that feeding by implanted tubes is a medical procedure with inherent risks and possible side effects, instituted by skilled healthcare providers to compensate for impaired physical functioning which analytically was equivalent to artificial breathing using a respirator." Justice Sandra Day O'Connor, in a concurring opinion, argued that whether or not a feeding tube is considered "medical treatment," it does require "a degree of intrusion and restraint" and that therefore "requiring a competent adult to endure such procedures against her will burdens the patient's liberty, dignity, and freedom to determine the course of her own treatment. Accordingly, the liberty guaranteed by the Due Process Clause must protect, if it protects anything, an individual's deeply personal decision to reject medical treatment, including the artificial delivery of food and water." Even the dissenting opinion drafted by Justice William Brennan and joined by Justices Thurgood Marshall and Harry Blackmun concluded that "no material distinction can be drawn between the treatment to which Nancy Cruzan continues to be subject—artificial nutrition and hydration—and any other medical treatment."

It was not legal reasoning and prior court decisions alone that led the justices to this conclusion. The opinions cited reports from major medical associations (the American Medical Association, American Academy of Neurology) and federal agencies (the Federal Drug Administration, Office of Technology Assessment) as well as a presidential commission and articles in major ethics journals. Furthermore, the justices wrote as though they were declaring the obvious, merely giving legal recognition to a consensus view. Chief Justice Rehnquist's passing reference to the "emotional significance of food" indicates that the Court was dismissive of the idea that removing a feeding tube was qualitatively different from unplugging a machine. The response to Terri Shiavo's case suggests that the public is not as certain as the Court on this matter.

Terri Schiavo: Politicizing Death

No end-of-life dispute comes close to the case of Theresa Marie Schiavo for its duration, the number of legal proceedings it generated, the involvement of third parties (politicians, religious leaders, commentators, media), or the use of modern means of communication (especially the Internet) to keep the case before the public eye. Fifteen years passed between Terri's cardiac arrest on February 25, 1990, and her death on March 31, 2005. Numerous legal proceedings in district, state, and federal venues produced mountains of documents and judicial opinions. Two laws were passed, one by the Florida legislature and one by the US Congress, specifically to interrupt a court order to allow the removal of Terri's feeding tube. National figures from President George W. Bush and his brother Florida governor Jeb Bush to Jesse Jackson and Ralph Nader entered the fray at various points. Websites offered perspectives from every angle and even became a part of the arguments through the posting of video clips of the incapacitated patient.

There is no need to rehearse the details of the tortuous path this case took. Michael Schiavo, Terri's husband, and one of his lawyers, Jon B. Eisenberg, have written books arguing their side, and the Schindlers, Terri's mother and father, have published their own account. The legal opinions in the case as well as commentaries from every imaginable interest group and private party are readily available on the Internet. As one who has made a point of following most of this documentary trail, I can confirm that anyone interested in the "blow-by-blow" has ample resources at his/her fingertips. It is essential, however, that I make clear what I believe are incontrovertible facts in this sad story, even though I know full well that not everyone will agree. First, and most important, the damage done to Terri's brain as a result of her heart stopping was catastrophic, irreversible, and so complete that any claim that she was aware of her surroundings or capable of any form of communication was demonstrably false. Any doubt on this matter was eliminated after an autopsy irrefutably documented the scale of cortical injury, but there was never any evidence to the contrary from any reputable source even before Terri died. Highly selective video clips and fanciful reports of interaction with Terri manufactured medical doubt where there was none among physicians sufficiently qualified in neurology to render an informed opinion. The fundamental error of those who wished to continue Terri's life was a failure to acknowledge a medical reality: "Awareness requires wakefulness, but wakefulness can be present without awareness" (Multi-Society Task Force 1994, 1501).

It is also a fact that no case involving a request to remove life support has ever received as many judicial reviews with such consistent findings as this one. The insistence on the part of the Schindlers and their supporters that Terri's due process rights were violated by an activist judiciary intent on authorizing their daughter's death is just not believable given the number of opportunities they had to make their arguments and the extreme care evident in each judicial decision. They lost, time and time again, on the merits of the case and not because of any kind of judicial impropriety. The cold reality is that the applicable laws (state and federal) were clear, there were ample precedents, and the medical testimony about Terri's condition was irrefutable. The only legitimate point of contention was whether the evidence of Terri's prior wishes reached the standard of "clear and convincing," but no appeal succeeded in persuading any judge to reverse the original court's judgment on that matter.

There is a third certainty in the Schiavo case: public surveys after Terri's death show that an overwhelming majority (84 percent) of Americans support right-to-die laws and almost three-quarters (74 percent) believe it is the right of close family members to make life-and-death medical decisions on behalf of a terminally ill relative (Pew Research Center 2006). These attitudes have changed little since 1990, suggesting an impressive stability in public opinion on these end-of-life issues. The same survey evidence points to strong majorities disapproving of the actions taken in response to the Schiavo case by Governor Jeb Bush, the Florida legislature, and the US Congress.

If Terri was in an irreversible vegetative state, if the courts had provided the Schindlers with sufficient opportunity to reverse the original judgment against them, and if most Americans agree with right-to-die laws, then why did the Schiavo case get so much attention? The answer is that this dispute was ultimately based on a disagreement not about evidence and law but about ideological positions on the boundaries of life. On one side was a well-organized and powerful religious right insisting on its version of the sanctity of life, from conception to a God-determined death. On the other side was an eclectic blend of advocates for the right to die and for the balance of powers between the three branches of government (executive, legislative, and judicial). Who joined which camp was not entirely predictable: a conservative and deeply religious Florida judge, George W. Greer, was the source of the original opinion granting Michael Schiavo the right to remove Terri's feeding tube while Democratic senator and former vice presidential candidate Joe Lieberman joined Republicans in passing the congressional act supporting the Schindlers' position. Who would ever have thought that African American political activist Jesse Jackson and consumer advocate and third-party presidential candidate Ralph Nader would stand side by side with anti-abortion crusader Randall Terry (recall his involvement in the Cruzan case) in demanding that Terri's feeding tube be reinserted (see Figure 3.1)?

The battle gained national attention for several reasons. First, the evangelical wing of the Republican Party had come a long way from its political status

Figure 3.1
Reverend Jesse Jackson speaks to the media, accompanied by Terri
Schiavo's family in front of the Woodside Hospice, Pinellas Park,
Florida, on March 30, 2005.
By permission, © Carlos Barria/Reuters/Corbis

during the Cruzan case. It now had believers and sympathizers in the highest positions of state and federal government, in part because of its financial resources and organizing ability during close elections. With conservative Republicans controlling Congress and the White House, a sympathetic and deeply religious Florida governor whose brother was president (see Jeb Bush quote at the start of the chapter), and a growing number of equally conservative judges gaining high-level appointments, the religious right considered it time to force a biblically based social agenda. The crusade to "save Terri" was the perfect opportunity to muster conservative forces and enrich political coffers, or so thought the leaders of major evangelical organizations and their political allies.

A second significant factor was that the case tested American notions of the bonds of kinship in a fashion that was tailor-made for sensationalistic reporting. Here was a husband, now living with another woman and having a child with her, pitted against the parents and siblings of his young wife. The law may give greater weight to persons related by marriage (affinal relations, in anthropological terms) than to biological kin (consanguineal relations), but high rates of divorce[5] and marital infidelity may leave the American public uncertain about the wisdom of this preference. It was all too easy to transform Terri's story into a morality play about an unfaithful husband anxious to dispose of his inconvenient wife while devoted parents fight to keep their innocent daughter alive. Note that this dynamic was not in play for Nancy Cruzan, whose family was undivided.

And then there were those videos. Still photographs of Nancy Cruzan, with her bloated face and twisted arms, spoke to the hopelessness of her condition. The brief segments of video the Schindlers posted on their website, by contrast, seemed to show a disabled but expressive young woman. To the untrained eye, unfamiliar with the appearance of a person in a VS, it was hard not to credit Terri with consciousness as she apparently smiled and reacted to a passing balloon. I showed these clips to students in an advanced seminar on medical ethics, triggering a debate that challenged a previous consensus that Michael Schiavo should have the right to withdraw Terri's feeding tube. The images spoke powerfully, even though they were deliberately edited from much longer recordings that conveyed a very different impression, according to judges and doctors.

The power of the political right, questions about the bonds of matrimony, and a persuasive video take us a long way toward understanding why the Schiavo dispute drew such unprecedented attention. However, I'd like to add one other reason to the mix: Americans' continuing ambivalence about the moral status of medically mediated feeding. Even though the US Supreme Court's Cruzan decision firmly established for legal purposes the equation between ANH and any other form of life support, the rhetoric of the Schiavo case demonstrates that segments of the general public remain unconvinced. Just as the protestors outside the hospital where Nancy Cruzan lay dying demanded that she not be starved, so did the assembled crowds awaiting Terri Schiavo's death insist that food and drink are the least we owe to a fellow human being. And I don't think it was only the protestors who found this path to death disquieting; we may, under normal circumstances, be expected to breathe on our own, but being fed is the primordial human experience of love and care.

The Problem with Miracles

There is a strong medical consensus about the vanishingly small chance that an adult in a prolonged VS will ever recover, and even in those rare cases a relapse into unconsciousness is very common. However, there are exceptional cases—often characterized as miraculous—of a return to at least partial awareness even after periods in variously defined states of unconsciousness. A good example is University of Arizona student Sam Schmid, who suffered massive brain injuries in a car crash on October 19, 2011, and was assumed to be near death. Then, just before Christmas two months later, he suddenly began responding to doctors' commands and proceeded to regain the ability to talk and walk. His mother is quoted as saying, "I do think of it as a miracle. He was so close to death and came back. I do believe God has a huge part in this" (James 2014).[6]

A more dramatic case is that of Arkansas resident Terry Wallis, who also suffered catastrophic brain damage in a car accident and for nineteen years was in a state variously described as a coma, a persistent vegetative state, and a minimally conscious state. Then, "Terry 'woke up' on June 11th of 2003, almost two decades after he lost consciousness. With no warning whatsoever, he began to speak" (The Terry Wallis Fund n.d.).

These and other "miracle stories" are included on right-to-life websites, such as New York State Right to Life (www.nysrighttolife.org/coma_recovery) and American Life League (www.all.org). They are potent narratives in the battle against removing ANH because they point to the uncertainty in VS diagnoses and invoke the culturally compelling command, "Never give up hope!" They also pit God's will against medical science by dramatic plot twists in which doctors were ready to declare death until a miraculous turn of events brought the patient back to consciousness. These are resurrection stories with a strong Christian lesson about the consequences of putting life-and-death decisions in human hands. They resonate with a solid majority of Americans, who believe miracles can cure VS patients (Green 2014).

There are problems with miracles. First, despite the media appeal of headlines like "Christmas Miracle" in the case of Sam Schmid, sometimes the facts point to predictable variation in outcomes, especially when the patient's unconscious time was less than three months (Schmid) or when the diagnosis of a "minimally conscious state" has replaced "persistent vegetative state" (Wallis). Recovery may not have been predicted in a particular case, but applying the loaded word "miracle" may be an overstatement, given what is known in medicine about the range of potential outcomes.

Miracle stories also tend to leave quite a lot out of the accounts. For example, for every one of the cases in which a VS patient regained some level of consciousness, how many patients are there who never improve? These patients don't get headlines, but they constitute the vast majority of VS cases of long duration. What is the level of continuing impairment for those who "recover," and how much ongoing care is required to maintain some progress in rehabilitation or even to preserve the patient's recovered abilities? What is the emotional burden carried by family members who are persuaded by the miracle stories that their relative in a VS will recover, when the likelihood is that there will be no happy ending? These are complications that get in the way of appealing stories of unexpected returns from death's door.

The final problem with VS miracle stories is that they downplay the physical impact of attempting to perpetuate biological life after prolonged unconsciousness. An excellent review of the debate about removing ANH notes that recent empirical evidence challenges the widely shared assumption that it is more "ordinary care" than "medical treatment":

> Evidence from observational studies showed that in general, ANH was futile for terminally ill patients, including those with advanced dementia. No evidence showed extension of life or improved quality of life with ANH, but considerable evidence indicated a high risk of bothersome complications—aspiration pneumonia, need for physical restraints, nausea, increased respiratory secretions, diarrhea, edema, and need for burdensome laboratory monitoring (Brody et al. 2011, 1054–1055).

This evidence leads some to argue that we should replace the phrase ANH with "forced feeding" and question the default assumption that patients, were they able to voice their wishes, would necessarily accept it. Advocates of this position point out that current standards of palliative medicine state that ANH should be avoided because it complicates the metabolic and biochemical changes in a dying patient that reduce appetite due to diminished ability to utilize nutrients. It is, in the words of psychiatrist Linda Ganzini, "counterpalliative" (Ganzini 2006).

The VS miracle stories have served the opponents of ANH removal in much the same way as Brittany Maynard's compelling videos have for supporters of PAD. Both engage a wider public in ethically complicated end-of-life decisions with emotional personal narratives that draw upon important cultural values, the right of self-determination for Maynard and the religiously inspired notion of hope in the accounts of Schmid and Wallis. Unfortunately the public relations value of these narratives can also hinder the kind of critical assessment that death disputes deserve.

In the Wake of Quinlan, Cruzan, and Schiavo

It would be easy to conclude from a review of the three most public disputes over VS that not much has changed in American attitudes in the intervening decades. In the Schiavo case we hear echoes of arguments and even repeat performances by some of the protagonists from the Cruzan and Quinlan trials. But it would be a mistake to overstate the continuities; a great deal has changed in the way Americans think about medically mediated dying, even as persistent disagreements arise in each new conflict over death decisions. It is also important to keep the high-profile battles in perspective. Physicians routinely withhold or withdraw life support measures and smooth the dying process for VS and other patients with a sensitive approach to pain management, ending many thousands of lives each year peacefully and without family discord or legal proceedings.

There have been significant strides since Quinlan in the promotion of living wills (also known as advance directives) as legal documents that guide decisions when a person is unable to communicate his/her wishes. Since first suggested by American attorney Louis Kutner in 1969, every state has approved forms for advance directives and/or health care proxy designations.[7] The variability of these documents and the laws that authorize them led to the drafting of the "Uniform Health Care Decisions Act" (1993) by the National Conference of Commissioners on Uniform State Laws, an association of state representatives that works to standardize critical legislation across the country. There is reason to hope that over time more states will adopt the draft act so that Americans won't have to worry that an advance directive from one state won't be accepted in another.

Interest in living wills/advance directives spiked as the Schiavo case progressed, with some websites that offer free forms reporting impressive increases in traffic, but most estimates still put the number of Americans who have completed the document at less than 20 percent. This virtually guarantees that there will continue to be occasional cases of families disagreeing about what an incapacitated relative would have wanted, and some of these will find their way into the courts. Injuries to the brain that result from accidents, violent attacks (especially with guns), and cranial aneurisms (strokes) will continue to create the conditions for these disputes because they occur suddenly, at various ages, and can result in severely compromised cognition. The Brain Injury Association reports that there are 1.4 million traumatic brain injuries each year in the United States, 235,000 of which require hospitalization. At least some of these cases are potential sources of conflict like that seen in the Quinlan, Cruzan, and Schiavo cases.

Even though there is now solid legal precedent, all the way to the US Supreme Court, for treating ANH as another medical treatment that surrogates may order withdrawn or withheld, the Schiavo case triggered counter-measures and ethical reconsiderations. In the aftermath of Schiavo a number of American states, including New York, Arizona, Oklahoma, and South Dakota, passed laws that differentiate ANH from other medical treatments and restrict the rights of surrogates to order removal. The position of the Catholic Church on the matter also shifted after Schiavo. As Brody and colleagues (2011) argue, a longstanding Church view that ANH was "extraordinary care" that families could morally consider excessively burdensome and have withdrawn was called into question by recent popes, including John Paul II, who called it "euthanasia by omission." More recently, guidance from the US Conference of Catholic Bishops in 2009 included an exception for the withdrawal of ANH if it is not prolonging life while imposing physical suffering (cited in Brody et al. 2011). The Catholic position seems to be evolving, but the Schiavo case certainly had an impact on Church teaching.

In sum, the question of whether removing ANH is the same as withdrawing any other medical treatment remains a point of contention, despite a strong consensus from the courts and medical experts that it is equivalent to other medical interventions. The Schiavo case contributed to the continuation of the debate, but I think there are also wider cultural reasons for its persistence. When presented as "food and water," ANH seems, to many Americans, as the least we owe to the critically ill. Legal reasoning and medical evidence is an anemic response to such a powerful cultural script. The following chapter will show that medicine and law also run up against culturally framed intuitions in the application of a brain death diagnosis, with consequences similar to those evident in the arguments over ANH and VS.

The Forecast

Whatever cultural norms may influence the response of families to a relative in a VS, increasing medical knowledge about the diagnosis and prognosis for this condition has removed some of the scientific uncertainty that prevailed when Karen Quinlan collapsed. There are far better guidelines for doctors to follow in differentiating temporary comas, minimally conscious states, and persistent vegetative states. The development of the Glasgow Coma Scale and the Coma Recovery Scale–Revised have helped to standardize diagnoses. More longitudinal evidence on VS patients has improved predictions of recovery.

That said, it is likely that errors in diagnoses and prognoses will continue to occur, either because of medical mistakes or simply because we are only beginning to understand how well the brain sometimes manages, over time, to establish new pathways for those that are damaged. The rare cases of recovery from disorders of consciousness will continue to grab public attention with headlines about medical miracles, and these will make surrogates' decisions all the more difficult. Although I am confident that most cases will be resolved in a fashion that is emotionally satisfactory to family members and that legal suits will continue to fold ANH into the category of medical treatments that may be withdrawn, I also expect that there will be more high-publicity cases that will keep the issue—and VS patients—alive.

I also expect that the religious right will continue to intervene in cases of disputed dying decisions. Given their messianic worldview and their absolute conviction that life of any sort is sacred—with the exception of some criminals and many enemies of the United States—there is no chance that the most conservative evangelicals will cease efforts to overturn right-to-die legislation and to halt medically managed dying. Whether or not they are successful will be determined by how effective they are at the ballot box. The majority of Americans who disagree with the extreme position of the evangelicals should not feel particularly reassured by the outcome of the Schiavo case; but for a very few votes in several appeals courts, the outcome could have been very different.

There is another aspect of the care of VS patients that will certainly continue. The difficulty faced by the Quinlan and Cruzan parents and by Michael Schiavo when they had to set aside their wish to keep their loved ones with them, when they had to stop believing there was some hope for recovery, will always subject families to the same hard choices. The complicated liminality created by our medical technology is every bit as hard to negotiate for families today as it was for those who have already faced this challenge, and I doubt that anything will diminish that dilemma in the future. Knowing when holding on is more for the sake of the living than for the benefit of the dying will remain the toughest hurdle on the way to releasing a relative to final death.

Chapter 4

Dead?

Brain-Dead Woman Dies After Giving Birth

A brain-dead woman who was kept alive for three months so she could deliver
the child she was carrying was removed from life support Wednesday and died,
a day after giving birth. ("Brain-Dead Woman" 2005)

It shouldn't be hard to differentiate the dead from the living, should it? The
Hollywood last gasp, eyelids gently closed by a loving relative or friend, white
sheet pulled over the body—it isn't all that complicated, is it? But whether
someone is certainly and irrevocably dead has been a source of debate since our
most distant ancestors were able to argue about the matter. Modern medicine's
capacity to keep a dead person alive isn't making it any easier.

Susan Torres, a twenty-six-year-old researcher at the National Institutes of
Health, officially died in May 2005 as a result of a stroke caused by a melanoma
in her brain. That is, she was declared to be brain dead based on tests that showed
no activity in either her neocortex or brain stem. Because Susan was pregnant at
the time of her collapse, her husband, Jason, decided to keep her on life support
long enough to allow the fetus to develop to a point that it could survive. On
August 2 a twenty-six-week-old baby girl was surgically removed from Susan's
womb, and the next day the machines that had maintained vital systems in the
mother were shut down. The infant died on September 11 from complications
associated with a perforated intestine.

Mortal Dilemmas: The Troubled Landscape of Death in America, by Donald Joralemon, 59–74. © 2016
Left Coast Press, Inc. All rights reserved.

Did Susan Torres give birth? If so, who died in May? Can a cadaver be "kept alive" on "life support" and then, months later, die again, as the language from the Associated Press report suggests? When is dead, dead enough?

This chapter considers the complications of declaring someone dead, in historical and cross-cultural contexts as well as in the wake of the biomedical technologies that were applied to Susan Torres. I pay special attention to the 1968 invention of an unprecedented way to diagnosis death, by the lack of any brain activity, and to the recurrent dilemmas that this novel medical definition has occasioned. In the process I challenge the common-sense assumption that biological death is a natural fact, not shaped by cultural ideas in the same way as social death. It is not just the dying process that sparks disputes like those reviewed in the previous chapters; what we take as definitive signs of death are also contested in contemporary America.

"The Rumors of My Death Have Been Greatly Exaggerated" (Mark Twain)

The fear of being prematurely declared dead has triggered ingenious, sometimes revolting, responses from diverse cultures. For example, from ancient Greece to eighteenth-century Europe people demanded that burial be postponed long enough for putrefaction to begin, figuring that a decaying corpse was unlikely to come back to life. The German *Leichenhaus,* or hospital for the dead, provided space for the purportedly deceased to lie in repose, connected to a bell system that would announce any movement to the caretaker. False alarms related to the build-up of postmortem gases were frequent. Attempts to control the overwhelming odors with antiseptic fluids and floral displays were largely futile in these precursors of the modern-day funeral home.

Other cultures have also adopted the wait-and-see approach to death. The Torajans of Sulawesi (Indonesia) wrap their dead in layers of absorbent cloths and leave them in a corner of their houses for however long it takes to gather the necessary resources for a funeral, which can be many months. The person is not considered to have died until he/she is removed from the house. Torajans don't make many mistakes with their dead.

Various forms of physical assaults have been offered as confirming tests for a declaration of death. Tickling with a feather and testing for pupillary responses were relatively benign alternatives compared to burning an appendage, sticking pins under fingernails, and opening the chest to look for heart action. When

Figure 4.1
The Hasty Burial by Antoine Wiertz (1850).

the arteries were cut or the heart pierced, the test for death could itself cause death if it hadn't already happened.

Edgar Allan Poe explored our fear of being buried alive in his short story "The Premature Burial" (1850), and the Belgian painter Antoine Wiertz gave it a visual expression in the painting "The Hasty Burial," in which a coffin lid is pushed aside by a still-breathing dead man (see Figure 4.1). According to sources summarized by Kenneth Iserson in his monumental book *Death to Dust: What Happens to Dead Bodies* (1994), there was a solid foundation for this terror. Well-documented cases of postmortem discoveries of life show that some victims of mistaken death declarations were rescued and survived for years. To avoid such blunders, the Victorian-era Society for the Prevention of People Being Buried Alive promoted greater rigor in the science of death determinations. Creative casket designs with built-in alarm systems for the inappropriately interred emerged in the late nineteenth century but never quite caught on with the public.

The growing popularity of embalming practices in the late nineteenth and early twentieth centuries diminished the likelihood that a living person would end up six feet under, as the process requires that the body be drained of blood and then flooded with a preservative solution. Still, errors in death determinations continue. After a serious traffic accident in 1993 Sipho William Mdletshe, a twenty-four-year-old resident of Johannesburg, South Africa, spent two days in a metal box at the mortuary before he recovered enough to draw an attendant's attention (*Arizona Daily Star,* March 22, 1993). In 2002 paramedics in Brooklyn pronounced a seventy-seven-year-old woman dead only to have police forensic officers later determine that she was just unconscious (ABCNews, February 13, 2002).

More common than these sorts of mistakes are cases in which a person who is clinically dead is brought back to a fully functioning life. This most often occurs when hypothermia or drug overdoses are involved. For example, Anna Bagenholm, a twenty-nine-year-old Norwegian skier, fell into icy water and was submerged for more than an hour, her body temperature dropping below 57 degrees Fahrenheit (normal is 98.6 degrees). Although she was clinically dead, doctors slowly warmed her body while performing critical resuscitation techniques. She had a full recovery and reports that the only continuing effect is a tingling in her hands (BBC News, January 28, 2000).

In the best-selling *How We Die* (1993), surgeon Sherwin Nuland helps us understand why it's so hard to be sure about death:

> The experience of dying does not belong to the heart alone. It is a process in which every tissue of the body partakes, each by its own means and at its own pace. The operative word here is *process,* not *act, moment* or any other term connoting a flyspeck of time when the spirit departs. . . . The sequence of events by which tissues and organs gradually yield up their vital forces in the hours before and after the officially pronounced death are the true biological mechanisms of dying (Nuland 1993, 42).

The problem, of course, is that for everyone but the forensic specialist it is precisely the "flyspeck of time when the spirit departs" and not the gradual loss of "vital forces" that is of concern. We want to know with certainty that the person's spirit or soul—or whatever we may wish to call the unique animating force that constitutes a living human being—is irreversibly gone. We can't stand by waiting for the gradual process of biological dying, organ-by-organ, tissue-by-tissue, before treating the person as dead. For one thing, that process can now be artificially delayed for long periods of time, as in the case of Susan Torres. For another, we are asked to make important decisions based on an unambiguous determination of death. It isn't just a matter of whether to proceed with burial, as it was for past generations, but whether to authorize the removal of vital organs for life-saving transplantation surgery. For this, precision is required—as was long ago recognized by a group of specialists who met at Harvard to redefine the moment of death.

Death by Committee

On December 3, 1967, Dr. Christian Barnard, a South African surgeon, transplanted a heart from an accident victim into Louis Washansky, a fifty-five-year-old grocer who suffered from diabetes and advanced heart disease. Transplants of kidneys from living, closely related donors had been performed since 1954, but Barnard was the first to attempt a human heart replacement. Although Washansky survived for just eighteen days before dying from complications associated with tissue rejection, the operation earned Barnard international fame and photographic coverage in *Life* magazine. It also created a dilemma: because a heart could only be transplanted if blood was still circulating in the donor and because the standard at the time for death declarations was the absence of heartbeat, the surgery required the removal of a vital organ from a donor who was not, technically speaking, dead. Was Barnard complicit in the death of the donor, Denise Darvall, as her medical team stopped resuscitation efforts before she was legally dead so as to permit the transplantation of a healthy heart?

Less than a year later, in August 1968, a solution was offered by Harvard University's Ad Hoc Committee to Examine the Definition of Death. Dr. Henry K. Beecher, an anesthesiologist previously noted for an exposé of ethically questionable medical experiments, convened a distinguished group of doctors, scholars, and one lawyer to consider changes in how death is determined. This is how the committee explained its task:

> Our primary purpose is to define irreversible coma as a new criterion for death. There are two reasons why there is a need for a definition: (1) Improvements in resuscitative and supportive measures have led to increased efforts to save those who are desperately injured. Sometimes these efforts have only a partial success so that the result is an individual whose heart continues to beat but whose brain is irreversibly damaged. The burden is great on patients who suffer permanent loss of intellect, on their families, on the hospitals, and on those in need of hospital beds already occupied by these comatose patients. (2) Obsolete criteria for the definition of death can lead to controversy in obtaining organs for transplantation. (Ad Hoc Committee 1968)

There is good reason to believe that the order of priorities was actually the reverse and that the committee's primary objective was to remove a troublesome constraint on a rapidly developing transplantation science. It must have occurred to the members that a benevolent concern for the well-being of the coma patient and his/her family sounded better than an admission that they were gerrymandering the definition of death to permit the removal of organs from persons whose hearts were still beating.[1] They concluded that a person should be considered "dead" if there is "no discernible central nervous system activity," even if mechanical-assist devices are maintaining blood circulation and respiration. This definition, which came to be known as "whole brain death," was eventually incorporated into the federal Uniform Death Determination Act (1981) as drafted by the President's Commission for the Study of Ethical Problems in Medicine and Biomedical and Behavioral Research.

For millennia, probably back to the earliest history of Homo sapiens, the absence of a heartbeat meant death, and occasional mistakes notwithstanding, it didn't take an expert to make the determination. The Harvard committee asked that we set aside wisdom born of the deepest convention and accept that the brain, not the heart, is the most vital organ. To paraphrase the French philosopher René Descartes, "I don't think, and therefore I'm not." And what's more, the committee made death a matter of expert opinion, not lay judgment.

What the committee did not do was tread into even more controversial waters by establishing death criteria that would have included persons in vegetative states. Although the article that published their recommendation was titled, "A Definition of Irreversible Coma," the committee actually chose to exclude from their new death diagnosis persons whose brain stem remained intact, despite complete loss of cortical function. None of the VS patients we discussed in the last chapter would fall under the committee's death definition, but we'll see that some of the same issues in those cases reappear when the notion of brain death is applied.

Some ethicists and social scientists have suggested that this momentous shift in the criteria for death occasioned surprisingly little public response in the United States, as compared to the resistance to the idea of brain death that later developed in some other countries, most notably Japan. I don't agree. There was so much on the public agenda in this country in the late 1960s and early 1970s that a seemingly arcane medical debate could go largely unnoticed. Think of the civil rights and women's rights movements, the environmental movement, the protests against the Vietnam War, the social turmoil associated with the use of psychedelic drugs, and the promotion of sexual freedom linked to the availability of contraception. Also recall that transplantation medicine was still in its infancy, making it unlikely that many family members would be asked to donate the organs of a relative now considered dead by brain criteria. It wasn't until the discovery of immunosuppressant drugs in the early 1980s that transplantations became routine medical practice, requiring larger numbers of donors. Finally, we need to remember that the new death definition was not instantly adopted, either legally or as a matter of common clinical practice, which further blunted whatever social impact it might have had.

We shouldn't mistake the absence of an immediate and large-scale protest against the Harvard committee's proposal for a willing acceptance on the part of medical workers and the American public. Medical ethicists still argue about the scientific, philosophical, and moral underpinnings of the brain death concept, and physicians raise troubling questions about the empirical claims on which the distinction between whole and partial brain death is based. Even today those on the front line of brain death determinations—emergency room doctors, neurologists, and nurses—report conflicting emotions when they maintain life support for a brain-dead patient solely for the sake of acquiring organs for another person. Anthropologist Margaret Lock (2002) reports that some critical-care nurses continue to talk to the patient who has been declared brain dead "just in case the soul is still there." The following cases demonstrate similar levels of ambivalence and confusion about brain death among the general public.

Brain Death Disputes

The year 2013 was notable for the emergence of two public controversies over brain death in the United States. The first brought attention to the incompatibility of a Texas state law designed to extend personhood protections to fetuses and a brain death diagnosis applied to a pregnant woman. The second pitted a mother of a thirteen-year-old against a California hospital that may have been responsible for the cascading complications that left the child with profound brain damage. Both cases summoned the same religiously inspired arguments about protecting life that we saw play out in the troubled history of Nancy Cruzan and Terri Shiavo but in a way that even more dramatically opposed medicine and religion because they focused on persons already declared dead. If the VS cases raised doubts about medicine's right to hasten death based on a *prognosis* of futility, these confronted medicine's right to act on a *diagnosis* of brain death.

Marlise Muñoz versus John Peter Smith Hospital

Early in the morning of November 26 thirty-three-year-old Marlise Muñoz had gone to the kitchen to prepare a bottle for her infant son when she collapsed from what doctors subsequently determined was probably a blood clot in her lungs. She lay on the floor for an hour without breathing before her husband, Erick, found her and, applying his paramedic training, began cardio-pulmonary resuscitation (CPR). She was transported by ambulance to Fort Worth's John Peter Smith Hospital (JPSH), where emergency staff sought in vain to save her life. That same day—Thanksgiving Day—she was declared brain dead.

If Marlise had agreed to be an organ donor or if her husband gave his consent, her body would have been kept on life support until arrangements were made for the harvesting of her organs. In the absence of consent to donate, the hospital would ordinarily have removed life support and transported the body to the morgue. But there was a complication: she was fourteen weeks pregnant. JPSH doctors explained to Erick that a section of the Texas Health and Safety Code (Section 166.049) prohibits the withdrawal or withholding of life-sustaining treatment from a pregnant woman and that they would, therefore, not take Marlise off the devices that were keeping her heart pumping and blood flowing. To do otherwise, they argued, would subject the physicians and the hospital to homicide charges, because the Texas Penal Code § 1.07 defines murder as intentionally causing the death of an "individual," a legal term that in Texas explicitly includes "an unborn child at every stage of gestation from fertilization until birth."

Predictably, Erick sued JPSH on the grounds that neither legal statute required preserving biological systems in a dead woman to protect a fetus. The Tarrant County Court ruled in Erick's favor on January 24, 2014, noting that a finding of death consistent with one part of the Texas Health and Safety Code made the subsequent provision regarding preserving the life of a pregnant woman inapplicable. State District Judge R. H. Wallace ruled that "Mrs. Muñoz is dead" and ordered the removal of all "life sustaining treatment from the body of Marlise Muñoz no later than 5:00 pm., Monday, January 27th, 2015" (Muñoz 2015). The hospital complied.

Local and national news organizations, including the *New York Times* and CNN, picked up this story, and right-to-life organizations joined in protesting in print, online, and in person at the courthouse. Pro-life advocates, including Operation Rescue's Troy Newman, used the language of "killing" and "crimes" and invoked the value of even disabled lives. Not unreasonably, they also pointed out that in other cases—like Susan Torres—pregnant women diagnosed as brain dead had been medically supported to give the "unborn baby" a chance to live. The fact that Marlise's fetus was known to have deformities incompatible with life did not diminish the intensity of the rhetoric opposing Erick's surrogate decision.

The hospital's choice to maintain Marlise on life support might, at first glance, seem peculiar. For a nonreligiously affiliated hospital—JPSH is a publicly funded nonprofit organization—to advance an argument in court that privileged the interests of the "unborn child" against the liberty and privacy interests of a patient and the fully legal right of a surrogate to make decisions on her behalf is exceptionally unusual. JPSH may have been opting for the path least likely to result in the hospital being held legally liable, but to do so when it meant contradicting the patient's interests and forcing treatment on a dead body is profoundly problematic as a matter of basic medical ethics.

We get closer to understanding the hospital's position if we remember that medical institutions do not exist in a political vacuum. Just a few months before this incident the Texas state legislature passed one of the most restrictive abortion laws in the country after a nationally publicized battle that included state Senator Wendy Davis, D-Fort Worth, engaging in a ten-hour-long filibuster against the measure. Governor Rick Perry stepped into the fray when he called the legislature back into special session so the measure could be approved, despite Davis's efforts. I suspect JPSH made a calculated decision not just about the risk of liability but also about the potential financial repercussions for a publicly funded hospital that exposed itself to the force of the pro-life lobby in a very conservative state. It may be significant that JPSH did not appeal the Tarrant County Court ruling; that decision gave the hospital the political cover it needed to act in the way it should have at the outset but without incurring the wrath of the religious right.

Beyond the politics of the situation, it is worth noting that the very legitimacy of the brain death diagnosis was called into question by the pro-life protestors. It was not just an "unborn baby" that would be murdered by the removal of life support; Marlise herself would also be the victim of medical killing according to the views opponents defended in the public arena. Even the other side showed signs of confusion about brain death. An editorial in the *Dallas Morning News* (January 9, 2014) was titled, "Let Marlise Muñoz Die." But by definition she was already dead. These are symptoms of a medical concept that has yet to gain public understanding and support.

Jahi McMath and a Mother's Doubt

On December 9, 2013, medical staff at the University of California San Francisco Benioff Children's Hospital (BCH) in Oakland, California, performed a tonsillectomy and adenoidectomy on a thirteen-year old African American, Jahi McMath, to resolve her sleep apnea. Profuse bleeding from her nose and mouth during recovery quickly led to a heart attack due to blood loss. A long resuscitation effort reestablished a heartbeat with the assistance of a ventilator, but Jahi's brain had been deprived of oxygen for so long that, on December 12, she was declared brain dead. A week later her mother, Latasha Winkfield, filed suit to stop BCH from disconnecting Jahi from the ventilator. She did not accept that Jahi was dead and told reporters that God may "spark her brain awake." She said that Jahi would only be dead when her heart stopped.

Judge Evelio Grillo of the Alameda County Superior Court heard testimony on December 24, including from Dr. Paul Fischer, chief of pediatric neurology at Lucile Packard Children's Hospital in Stanford, California, who confirmed the brain death determination. Although the judge declined the family's request to force BCH to maintain life support, he continued a restraining order to give the family a chance to appeal. Ultimately the US District Court for the Northern District of California also denied the family's petition but permitted negotiations to arrange for a nonaffiliated doctor to do the procedures necessary for Jahi to be transferred to another facility. On January 5, 2014, she was flown by a private air ambulance service to a clinic in New Jersey, where she remains as of this writing. The foundation established by Terri Schiavo's family is credited with helping to finance the move.

The next step in the ongoing legal proceedings came in October 2014 when Jahi's mother, Latasha Winkfield, petitioned the Alameda Superior Court to reverse the BCH declaration of brain death on the grounds that both she and three neurosurgeons were prepared to testify that Jahi was improving and that she never was actually dead. The court reappointed the same physician it had heard from in the first suit, Dr. Fischer, who reaffirmed his previous judgment after considering the new evidence. Winkfield's lawyers requested and were granted a postponement pending the acquisition of testimony from international experts.

Some commentators have suggested that there may have been a financial consideration behind the request to void Jahi's brain death declaration, potentially significant given that on March 2, 2015, the family filed a medical negligence suit against BCH and the doctor who cared for her. In California there is a cap on damages in medical negligence suits if a child is dead but not for a child who suffered serious harm but is still alive.[2] In the latter case a suit can include ongoing medical costs that greatly exceed the cap in cases that resulted in death. An additional legal twist is that New Jersey, where Jahi is now residing, is one of only two states (New York is the other) that provides an exception to brain death declarations based on a family's religious objection.[3]

Los Angeles Times columnist Meghan Daum titled a December 21, 2013, editorial "Jahi McMath, Alive in Social Media" (Daum 2013). She documented the proliferation of Jahi-related Twitter posts, both favorable to and critical of the family, as well as the emergence of websites established to fundraise on Jahi's behalf. Not mentioned in Daum's piece was the Facebook page "Keep Jahi Mcmath on Life Support," which had 32,123 "likes" as of early 2015. Although the courts may have been the primary arena for the legal battles, the public has also been weighing in with views that should be discomforting to those who believe brain death is a firmly established medical concept.

Bioethical Analyses of the Muñoz and McMath Cases

Professional bioethicists and others who routinely participate in public debates over ethical disputes in medicine responded quickly to these two cases of brain death. Particularly interesting in the resulting discussion is the divide between those who insist on the scientific foundation of brain death determinations and others who argue that brain death is not the same thing as biological death. The debate is important not just because it speaks to the conflicting views in the Muñoz and McMath cases but also because the presumed equivalence between brain death and biological death is the justifying rationale for proceeding with organ donations from individuals whose blood is still circulating due to assistive technologies. If brain death is not the same as biological death defined by traditional cardio-pulmonary criteria, then the potential donor is still alive and removing vital organs would constitute homicide.

The Uniform Death Determination Act (UDDA), originally drafted by the 1981 President's Commission for the Study of Ethical Problems in Medicine and Biomedical and Behavioral Research (President's Commission) and is now accepted by forty-four American states and the District of Columbia, asserts the equivalence between two means of defining death:

> An individual who has sustained either (1) irreversible cessation of circulatory and respiratory functions, or (2) irreversible cessation of all functions of the entire brain, including the brain stem, is dead. A determination of death must be made in accordance with accepted medical standards.

Behind the UDDA's dual standard for death determinations is the so called dead donor rule, which stipulates that organs may only be taken from someone who has been declared dead. Donation after a neurological determination of death—number two above—constitutes a primary source of transplantable organs because the continued circulation of blood made possible by assistive devices maintains the viability of those organs. If the cessation of brain functions were not accepted as a definition of death, then the dead donor rule would prohibit removal of organs from brain-damaged individuals until assistive devices are removed and the heart stops, at which point most of the organs would no longer be transplantable. The decision to withdraw assistive devices would also be made more ethically complicated because doing so would constitute intentionally ending a life rather than halting futile interventions for a dead person.

Ethicists have not considered the usefulness of brain death for the supply of organs as a sufficient argument for it to be equated with death defined by cardio-pulmonary criteria. Some other rationale was required to finesse the application of "dead" to a body that appears to be alive, thanks to the continued blood circulation facilitated by ventilators and heart monitors. Worse yet for those defending the medical validity of brain death was the discovery that some basic biological functions can continue even after near total loss of neural activity, including wound healing, spontaneous movements, maintaining a warm body temperature, fighting infections, and even, in a few cases, supporting the continued gestation of a fetus (Shaw 2015).

While the country was busy accepting the UDDA, brain death included, and physicians were applying the novel death criteria to thousands of patients, ethicists tried out a variety of rationales for equating new and old death definitions. There was the brain's role in the "integrative functioning of the organism as a whole" argument proposed by the President's Commission, followed by the "vital work of a living organism—the work of self-preservation, achieved through the organism's need-driven commerce with the surrounding world" offered by President George W. Bush's Council on Bioethics (2008).[4] Most recently, from neurologist James L. Bernat (2014), comes the "cessation of the organism as a whole," when the "organism has lost immanency . . . auto-finality . . . self-reference . . . [and] completeness and indivisibility" (citing Bonelli, Prat, and Bonelli 2009).

Critics are unimpressed. They understand the practical utility of a brain death determination but deny that it has the biological validity of death established after the end of blood circulation. In fact, they argue that brain death is a "legal fiction," which is when "something known to be false (or not known to be true) [is treated] as if it were true for a particular legal purpose" (Shaw 2015, 304). For example, the concept "legally blind" does not require that the person is, in fact, totally blind, only that for the purposes of such things as driver's licenses and disability claims, their sight is sufficiently impaired that they might just as well be blind (Truog and Miller 2014). Brian death, by this analysis, draws a false analogy to biological death established by cardio-pulmonary criteria because there are important social benefits that result from treating individuals with a loss of neural function as "dead enough." The legal fiction preserves scarce financial resources that would otherwise be wasted on hopeless cases, and it provides a fig leaf to physicians who want to provide viable organs for transplantation without being accused of murder.

Champions of brain death argue that there would be terrible repercussions if the concept were to be treated as a legal fiction rather than an unalterable biological fact. It would call into question the applicability of the dead donor rule and thereby jeopardize a major source of transplantable organs. It would encourage families to question the certainty of irreversibility, which would result in the needless expenditure of scarce health care dollars to maintain the biological functioning of bodies that should instead be on their way to the morgue. Decades of legal consensus, hard-won public approval, and standardized clinical practice would be called in question.

Opponents insist that the public has a right to know that brain death is not the same as biological death, determined on the basis of cardio-pulmonary criteria, and that greater transparency would actually improve communication between physicians and patient families.

> Changing the conversation among bioethicists and other professionals is the first step in becoming honest with the public about what it means to be deemed dead in accordance with neurological criteria and why it is appropriate to procure organs from individuals who are legally but not biologically dead. (Truog and Miller 2014, 13)

Regarding the potential impact on organ transplantation, two prominent critics assert (without any evidence to support their view): "We are doubtful that public support for transplantation depends on a belief that brain dead donors are biologically dead" (Truog and Miller 2014, 13). They also argue that applying a legal fiction model to brain death would focus attention on the most important issues: for Marlise Muñoz the right to consent to treatment and for Jahi McMath the right to a degree of flexibility for religious objections. They acknowledge that their proposal is unorthodox but plead with their interlocutors to confront the fact that brain death is not built on a biologically sound foundation.

Is Cardiac Death More "Real?"

Physicians and bioethicists treat organic facts as definitive indicators of death, and the arguments are simply over which facts count. Most consider the irreversible cessation of cardiac activity as the gold standard for death determination; it seems to be so clearly objective that all other criteria are compared to that ideal. For example, critics of brain death talk about death determinations based on loss of cardio-pulmonary functions as "biological death" and argue that because neurological criteria don't measure up to that standard, they must be considered legal fictions. But choosing to define death as what happens when the heart stops is no less arbitrary, no more objective—read "culture-free"—than any other set of biological criteria. As we saw in the quote from Sherwin Nuland, death is a process, not an event, and every cell has its own manner and time of expiration. Privileging cardiac arrest among the many biological signs of dying may be clinically convenient, but it is still a culturally informed convention.

The compelling nature of cardiac death determinations, the fact that listening for a heartbeat to establish whether someone has died has such a long history, requires that I provide additional demonstration to show how it is a cultural construction. Transplant medicine offers a good example. In an effort to recover more organs for transplantation, hospitals have adopted the so-called Pittsburgh Protocol. Named for the medical center that first proposed it, this procedure reinstates the old heart criteria for death but allows for preparations that speed the declaration of death and protect internal organs from deterioration due to loss of blood flow. Under the "controlled donation" variant of the protocol, a patient who is dependent on a cardiac assist device and who agrees to donation (or his/her surrogates agree) is moved to a surgical room. His/her body is prepped for organ removal by administering a solution that will slow cell loss when blood flow ceases. Then all assist devices are removed and the surgical team waits for the heart to stop. Assuming it does, no artificial resuscitation is attempted and a prescribed period of time is allowed to pass to assure that the heart does not begin to beat again on its own. At the appointed moment, usually just a matter of a few minutes, death is declared and the surgeon proceeds with organ removal.

Now this would appear to be a cardiac determination of death, but notice that it is fully orchestrated and that the amount of time allowed for the heart to spontaneously restart is justified primarily by the impact of interrupted blood flow for transplantable organs. Is five minutes of cardiac arrest enough to be declared dead, or can it be even less? The stop clock is set for the removal of organs, not for a neutral determination of death. Suddenly a cardiac definition of death is anything but an objective measure of a life ending.

It makes perfect sense that experts would try to find incontrovertible ways to define death, and it is also reasonable that they would turn to measurable biological functions to do so. But in the process they have deluded themselves into thinking that biologizing death frees the declaration from the imprint of culture, whether we are talking about cardiac or brain criteria. More importantly they have taken the meaning of death further and further from commonsense understandings.

What might Erick Muñoz and Latasha Winkfield think about the direction of bioethical debates centered on their loved ones? Would Erick puzzle over whether Marlise had residual biological functioning beyond her dead brain? Would Latasha find solace in the conclusion that Jahi's death was a legal fiction? I suspect that they would judge the academic interest in their families' tragedies unwelcome and misplaced. Like most people confronted with sudden loss, they probably had better grounded and more fundamental questions: Is the person I love still present in that body, and what would she want me to do?

In the Wake of Muñoz and McMath

It is worth taking stock of how these two tragic stories have affected the way death is managed in America, as we did after reviewing the VS cases in the previous chapter. We should begin by remembering that disputes over brain death declarations are rare. Although always emotionally complicated and not infrequently fraught with doubts on the part of family members, skillful doctors and nurses usually manage to help families navigate through the shock of a sudden death and even succeed in securing consent for organ donation about half the time. For a case to result in conflicts that earn headlines and court time, it has to touch on some very sensitive issues, either for the family or for a wider public ready to insert itself into the discussion, and it must somehow gain media attention. When these conditions are met, disagreements escalate into legal battles, and the whole story goes viral.

The lasting legacy of the Muñoz story is likely to be a renewed push to pass fetal protection laws like the Texas statute but with language that will extend to the prohibition against the removal of life support from a pregnant woman to include women who have been declared brain dead. Whether any such law would pass constitutional review in the courts is an open question, but if the extension of personhood protections to fetuses continues to gain legislative momentum, it seems likely that a judge will be asked to weigh the harm to a brain dead patient being kept "alive" against the state's interest in the life of the fetus. I would hesitate to predict the outcome of such a case.

The McMath case is more complicated. On the one hand, it provides another chink in the armor of brain death determinations and may encourage other states beyond New Jersey and New York to consider permitting religious exceptions. On the other hand, the public response to Jahi's situation was so divided that it is hard to imagine that the case represents a pivotal point in the way medicine manages patients with catastrophic loss of neural functioning. There may be a greater impact among African Americans, who already manifest higher levels of doubt about the medical profession than other segments of American society (Jacobs et al. 2006).

What is significant about these two cases for our purposes is that they show how even the declaration of death can be politicized and transformed into rallying points for causes well beyond the circumstances of the deceased and her/his family. It is largely, though not exclusively, the religious right that intervenes in brain death cases, as it has in public debates about physician-assisted death and vegetative states. Religiously grounded assumptions about the sacred value of all human life, from fertilized eggs to brain dead persons, drive opposition to abortion just as they motivate protests against "pulling the plug" at the other end of the life cycle. Ideas about "natural" processes and convictions about God's will are routinely set against medicine's scientific conclusions. If there is to be any progress in the troubled territory of dying and death in America, it will have to involve a more productive conversation between religion and medicine at the end of life than we have seen over the past several decades.

Before I shift the focus to dilemmas that arise after death, I offer an interlude of reflections on the choices we might make to address some of the issues I have reviewed in this chapter and the previous two. I want to make clear that in doing so I am stepping out of my role as anthropological observer and adopting the vantage point of an interested citizen. After this brief pause I'll put my anthropological hat back on and consider points of tension in America's approach to mourning.

Interlude

Reflections on Dying Dilemmas

The disputes about dying that have reached the general public over the past thirty years show a substantial consensus about the factors to be considered in death decisions: consciousness, prognosis, and suffering. At one extreme, the majority of Americans agree that when a complete loss of consciousness is coupled with no chance of recovery and needless suffering—even in the sense of a loss of human dignity—the subject is as good as dead. At the opposite extreme, few would want physicians and family to give up on someone with temporarily compromised consciousness, a reasonable chance for recovery, and manageable pain.

The space in between these extremes is the contested territory in death decisions. Degrees of uncertainty about a person's level of consciousness and/or prognosis reduce the likelihood that treatment will end. Even if the prognosis is certain, mixed evidence for consciousness or suffering can delay a death decision. For example, a person in the late stages of amyotrophic lateral sclerosis (ALS, or Lou Gehrig's Disease) has a terrible prognosis and may be suffering horribly but nonetheless retains consciousness and is not likely to be considered dead. Advanced Alzheimer's disease is marked by a virtually complete loss of cognitive capacity and a terminal prognosis but may not be associated with significant physical suffering. Patients in this state are typically kept alive until they succumb to a secondary disease that family and physicians choose not to treat (e.g., pneumonia). The decision to withhold treatment in these cases is an indication that at some point in the disease process death is considered preferable to a meaningless life.

Mortal Dilemmas: The Troubled Landscape of Death in America, by Donald Joralemon, 75–80. © 2016 Left Coast Press, Inc. All rights reserved.

We should remind ourselves that families manage to make difficult death decisions in most situations, even if the process requires emotional discussions and an empathetic medical staff. But it's also clear that we need to consider ways to avoid and/or resolve conflicts that do arise. I suggest three alternative approaches. The first two involve a loss of decision-making authority for families, either by the return to a medical model that grants that authority to doctors or through the perpetuation of the current reliance on the court system to mediate disputes. The third option would aim to facilitate conflict resolution through a program of dialogue and compromise in a nonjudicial forum. Let's take these options one at a time.

Death as a Medical Matter

There was a time in America when physicians were granted almost complete power to make treatment decisions for their patients, including when to withhold or withdraw therapies they judged futile. The patients' rights movement in the latter part of the twentieth century diminished medical authority through informed consent regulations and the threat of malpractice suits. This had a profound impact on the role of physicians in end-of-life decisions. Doctors still influence the direction of a family's deliberations—because they control the way a patient's condition is presented and are still granted a high degree of respect—but they are no longer in a position to make unilateral judgments about when a person is dead, or at least not without the potential for conflict with family.

Other highly developed countries have not subjected physicians to the same loss of authority, and as a result, end-of-life decisions continue to be treated as a doctor's responsibility. This is not to say that there aren't conflicts, especially when there is a disagreement among physicians about a patient's prognosis, but the jurisdiction for death decisions ultimately rests with doctors and not family members. The anthropologist Joan Cassell discovered this contrast when she compared intensive care units in the United States to one in New Zealand. At the latter site, "doctors presented decisions to move from cure to comfort care as unequivocal *medical* judgments" and simply waited until the family came around to accept their directions (Cassell 2005).

I doubt American physicians will ever regain the status of unquestioned authorities, although they may recover a more central role in limiting choices at the end of life through their gate-keeping function. This country continues to put doctors between patients and the insurance companies that pay the bills,

increasingly requiring medical professionals to introduce financial considerations into the treatment calculus for critically ill patients. What some have
called the "green screen" already influences the treatment options available
to patients without insurance or with coverage that includes deductibles and
spending limits. When the prognosis is poor and the price tag for continued
treatment is high, monetary considerations will become more pressing as "managed care" health insurance companies and for-profit hospitals strive to improve
their bottom lines. Unless there is a significant overhaul in America's health
care financing, doctors will increasingly be in the terrible position of equating
"as good as dead" with "unable to pay" and issuing orders accordingly. This is
not the kind of authority that I suspect most doctors would wish to accept or
that the American public would permit.

Death as a Judicial Affair

A society as diverse as the United States is unlikely to find consensus on highly
contentious issues, as the endless arguments over abortion demonstrate. In the
absence of a common ground we retreat to legislative and judicial mediation of
the disputes that divide us, assuming that our country's Constitution and Bill
of Rights provide the essential principles for successful arbitration. Even the
losers in these venues can hope that political action, as in the state and federal
legislation prompted by the Schiavo case, will give them yet another day in court.

But our reliance on the judicial system to resolve disputes about death has
unfortunate flaws and consequences. It can thrust families into adversarial
camps; even those who might otherwise have served as mediators between
disagreeing relatives are forced to choose sides. Doctors, families, and others
who choose to intervene in particular cases are encouraged to adopt a "take no
prisoner" approach to the legal proceedings and in the court of public opinion.
Judges with no medical training are required to assess competing scientific
claims from physicians about the patient's current condition and prognosis.
The appeal process can be used to delay a final resolution, often for extended
periods. Finally, litigating death shifts the focus from concern for the patient
to arguments about jurisdiction, evidence, and legal rights. This is clearly not
in the interest of the person over whom the battle is waged.

The courts are simply the wrong venue for dying and death determinations.
We already ask too much of our judicial system by demanding it referee other
tumultuous personal conflicts, from child custody to inheritance. As hard as
it may sometimes be, we shouldn't absolve ourselves from the responsibility

of deciding whether our loved one is close enough to death to let him/her go. There is something cowardly about turning over this ultimate decision to a stranger in a black robe.

Death as a Consultative Process

Physicians have used the concept of medical futility in the late stages of terminal illness as a bridge between intervention-based medicine and hospice-based palliative care. The extensive clinical and bioethical literature on the concept offers some guidance for a more constructive approach to potential disputes like those we have reviewed in the previous chapters. It focuses our attention on providing honest appraisals of medicine's limits while opening space for a conversation between physicians and the families of dying patients.

A wide range of definitions of medical futility have been proposed, but there is general agreement that effective communication and a structured decision process are at least as important as a precise definition (Joralemon 2002). Typically guidelines stipulate that doctors should explain the medical situation in lay terms, that empirical data must underpin the recommendation, and that the focus should be kept on what the patient would wish for him/herself, given the probable outcomes. If an impasse is reached, procedures usually call for a consultation with the hospital's ethics committee, which is trained in mediation techniques and includes both medical and community members. In roughly 4 percent of such cases no resolution results from these efforts. Guidelines then usually call for attempts to transfer the patient to a facility willing to follow the surrogates' wishes. If no facility can be found, most hospitals permit physicians to withdraw or withhold treatment even against the family's objections. At that point the litigation ball is in the surrogates' court.

We have to be clear about what medical futility means to patients and their families: it is effectively a death declaration. When a doctor announces that further treatment is useless, the threshold to social death is crossed and the waiting for biological death begins. It should come as no surprise that families might be reluctant to accept this determination, especially as it often comes from a physician with whom they have had little previous contact. The cultural myth of medical miracles creates false expectations and adds to suspicions that more could and should be done. A sympathetic process that recognizes how closely "medical futility" resembles "good as dead" to those on the receiving end of the news is certainly a step in the right direction. To make it work we need physicians who are willing to spend the time necessary to help the family across the decision threshold and to provide reassurance that care and comfort remain after interventions are halted.

What the medical futility approach allows is for surviving family to adjust to the reality of social death—"there's nothing more we can do"—before having to confront the full force of biological death—"your daughter/son/wife/husband is dead." Many doctors already adopt this incremental approach, releasing partial information over time, but there are also pressures that discourage a take-it-slow strategy. Critical care beds are scarce and costly, medical staff are often juggling untenable case loads, cultural barriers get in the way of effective communication, and desperate patients on transplant lists wait in the background. But haste can be costly over time, as parties dig in their heels, trust between families and medical staff evaporates, and more stakeholders demand attention.

At the heart of this consultation model is an openness to a more experience-near idea of death as the permanent cessation of personhood. Instead of a recitation of "biomarkers of death" (Peterson et al. 2014), the conversation with family members asks about the person in the hospital bed and about choices he/she would have made, knowing that medicine was out of options. The concept of personhood has been so thoroughly associated with the pro-life position on abortion that it may seem a poor choice as a structure for futility discussions. The passage of so-called fetal personhood laws in many states—including the statute that was at the center of the Muñoz case—marks the concept as politically divisive. However, we would be sticking our heads in the sand if we thought that the importance of personhood considerations in the way death is considered will go away by applying medical constructions that reduce the meaning of death to biological processes. If, instead, we recognize that death ultimately means the loss of a person, we are then able to ask more contextually significant questions about the meaning of medical information.

Personhood in Bioethics

The concept of personhood has a history in many bioethical debates, including those regarding death. It has been presented as an alternative to both brain and cardiac criteria for defining death. The idea is employed by scholars who believe the loss of neocortical functions, rather than all neural activity, is sufficient to declare death because cortical functions (e.g., consciousness, judgment, reasoning) define what it means to be a human person. "Loss of higher brain functions robs us of all that makes us human in any sense beyond that defined by our genetic endowment" (Botkin 1988, 252). If we can identify the traits that are quintessentially human—that make personhood possible—then the permanent loss of those traits should be sufficient to declare death.

That personhood definitions of death have not gained much traction is attributable to the kinds of arguments made by National Institute of Health bioethicist Seema Shah:

> No jurisdiction uses a personhood standard of death, and a shift to that standard would necessitate dramatic legal change. What counts as a person is already hotly contested. Given the controversy surrounding definitions of personhood, it is hard to imagine that a democratic process would adopt a personhood standard of death. Thus, a personhood standard of death is not the correct way to characterize the legal standard of brain death and is unlikely to provide much legal utility. (Shah 2015, 323)

Shah's logic is that because no current laws base death determinations on criteria related to personhood and because it is a contentious idea that would challenge democratic processes, it should not be pursued. The problem is that ideas about personhood are directly implicated in arguments about autonomy and physician-assisted death, about continued evidence of purposeful activity in conflicts over vegetative state patients, and about the validity of brain death declarations. When Brittany Maynard argued that her right of self-determination extended to choosing when and how to die, she was drawing upon a particular idea of the person as a rights-bearing entity. When Terri Schiavo's parents saw evidence of intentionality in her eye movements and facial gestures, they were affirming a view of consciousness as a core element in personhood. And when Latasha Winkfield rejected the death declaration for her daughter, she was asserting a commitment to the idea of life's sanctity, a conviction embedded in a religious view of the person as a child of God. Contentious or not, notions of personhood are central to the way we think about death and its defining characteristics.

Whatever the difficulties, and whether it can be enshrined in law, I think it is time to reconsider the value of personhood as a framework for meaningful discussions between doctors and the families of critically ill patients. This would take us away from the reductionist view of death as biology and draw medicine closer to the priorities of those it serves. There certainly will be disagreements about what constitutes the essential ingredients of personhood and about the protection of those most vulnerable, but at least those debates will be about something more important than residual biological functions after brain death. It is time to take personhood out of the shadows and put it front and center in the debates about when meaningful life has ended.

Chapter 5

Grief: Is It Complicated?

In the version of grief we imagine, the model will be "healing." A certain forward movement will prevail. The worst days will be the earliest days. . . . [We cannot] know ahead of the fact (and here lies the heart of the difference between grief as we imagine it and grief as it is) the unending absence that follows, the void, the very opposite of meaning, the relentless succession of moments during which we will confront the experience of meaninglessness itself. (Didion 2005, 188–189)

[Prolonged grief disorder (PGD)] is a state of chronic grieving that persists for 6 months or longer and is characterized by intense separation distress, intrusive and emotionally troubling thoughts about the deceased, a sense of meaninglessness, trouble accepting the loss, and functional impairment. (Holland et al. 2009, 190–201)

There is much to be done and many decisions to be made immediately after a death. To donate or not to donate? To cremate or bury? Open or closed casket? Funeral or memorial service? Grave markers? Disposition of cremains? There are family and friends to notify, an obituary to write, the last will and testament to find and send to probate court, accounts to close, notifications to government agencies (e.g., Social Security, Department of Veteran Affairs, Internal Revenue Service) to send. It can take a while for the urgency of final arrangements to subside and for the experience of loss to begin. We call that experience grief.

A concerted effort is afoot to treat some forms of grief as a disease. Researchers are accumulating evidence to distinguish normal, healthy grief from its alleged

Mortal Dilemmas: The Troubled Landscape of Death in America, by Donald Joralemon, 81–94. © 2016 Left Coast Press, Inc. All rights reserved.

pathological cousin, complicated grief (also known as prolonged grief disorder, bereavement-related depression, or traumatic grief). The former is what any ordinary person confronted with the loss of a loved one should experience. The latter is said to be something altogether different, a condition requiring medical attention and some not-yet-well-defined combination of psychological counseling and pharmaceutical treatment. Duration and intensity of symptoms are the primary criteria by which the two are differentiated by the psychiatrists who are promoting the new diagnosis.

In this scenario the clock starts when your loved one's death is declared. If you fail to adjust to your loss within the prescribed period and if the severity of symptoms are sufficiently serious, you may be a candidate for a diagnosis of complicated grief. There is no consensus on how long normal grief lasts, but if more than, say, six months have passed and you have yet to show signs of re-duced sadness and a reengagement with the social world, you may be considered sick. Handy self-report instruments—the Inventory of Complicated Grief, the Texas Revised Inventory of Grief, and the Hogan Grief Reaction Checklist—can gauge where your grief stands on a scale from normal to pathological.

The drive to medicalize some forms of grief has intensified in recent years as proponents sought to have the condition listed in the fifth edition of the *Diagnostic and Statistical Manual* (DSM-5) of the American Psychiatric Association. This bible for mental diseases has had a history of downplaying the symptoms associated with bereavement. Not until the fourth edition did they earn inclusion under the category of "Other Conditions That May Be a Focus of Clinical Attention." In the absence of a ready diagnostic pigeonhole, clinicians turn to a variety of alternative codes for patients they judge to be suffering abnormally from grief: adjustment disorder, dysthymic disorder, major depressive disorder, bipolar disorder, schizoaffective disorder, posttraumatic stress disorder, dissociative disorder, or borderline psychotic disorder. These diagnoses justify insurance claims for drugs and counseling sessions, but the associated treatments have been judged "resoundingly inefficacious," leading many to think that grief needs its own special label and specific treatment regimen.

The psychotherapist Jeffrey Kauffman thinks more is at stake than a DSM revision. He sees prolonged and unresolved grief as a symptom of a failed societal response to death, a "loss of the normativity of the human response to death [that is] catastrophic . . . a dominant sociocultural trend" (Kauffman 2008, 76). By implication, modern societies foster intensified unsettled grief because they no longer offer the bereaved the cultural frameworks and traditions that once structured mourning. Kauffman says that individual pathology in response to death is born of a "post traditional context." This should sound familiar; it is essentially the argument I outlined in the first chapter: somehow we have lost our way, culturally speaking, when it comes to death.

This chapter considers the merits of Kauffman's claim and assesses the idea that some kinds of grief should be seen as a treatable disease. I inject some historical and cross-cultural material into the discussion to see whether there is reason to believe we are culturally bankrupt in the face of bereavement. I also consider the push to medicalize grief in the broader context of medicine's management of life transitions. In the end, we should be in a better position to see whether grief is really all that complicated.

Terminological Matters

We should begin with some conceptual clarifications. The death literature defines the actual loss of a person to whom one is attached as "bereavement" and "grief" as the emotion this loss may engender. "Mourning" is the culturally patterned response to bereavement. These three concepts differentiate aspects of experience that are, in fact, intertwined. Bereavement is only distinct from the grief that accompanies it for the disinterested observer, and mourning rituals give form and substance to the inchoate swirl of emotions we call grief. Still, distinguishing bereavement from grief allows us to consider the relationship between the nature of the loss (e.g., how closely the survivors are tied to the deceased) and the intensity of the grief, just as separating the emotions of grief from the cultural scripts of mourning permits us to explore the relationship between individual and collective experience.

The concept of grief stages also deserves a bit of background. Elizabeth Kübler-Ross, in her classic book *On Death and Dying* (1969), identified a series of emotional steps taken by terminally ill persons as they adjust to the reality of their impending death: denial, anger, bargaining, depression, and acceptance. Professional counselors and lay people alike have applied variants of this framework to the experience of grief, sometimes replacing the idea of stages with the notion of psychological tasks that must be accomplished before someone can be said to have successfully adjusted to a loss. The individual going through the stages and achieving the tasks is said to be doing his/her "grief work." Consider how closely this idea resonates with the Protestant ethic! Grief is not so much an emotional experience as a job to be completed in a structured fashion and in an allotted time.

There are as many views of the ideal resolution of grief as there are counselors and theoreticians writing about it. One tradition, dating back to Sigmund

Freud's classic essay "Mourning and Melancholia" (1917), sees the goal of grief as the breaking of bonds to the deceased or the withdrawal of attachment to the "loved object." The psychiatrist Erich Lindemann, who coined the term "grief work" and distinguished normal from abnormal grief, described the task as "the emancipation from the bondage to the deceased, readjustment to the environment in which the deceased is missing, and the formation of new relationships" (Lindemann 1944).

There are many societies that seem to have taken Freud's view very seriously. The Wari' of Brazil's Amazon traditionally believed that the memory of the deceased must be obliterated for the family to be able to move forward and for the spirit of the dead to be integrated into a community of ancestor-animals. This meant the destruction of the deceased's home, belongings, and anything else that might remind the living of their dead kin or hold the deceased's spirit to its familiar world. Most dramatically, according to the anthropologist Beth Conklin (2001), the Wari' dismembered, cooked, and ate the body of the deceased so that his/her closest kin would have no visual memory that might impede the spirit's journey in the afterlife or complicate the survivors' adjustment to the death. For the Wari', funerary cannibalism was the most compassionate act the community could perform for the grief stricken.

An alternative theoretical approach, advanced by sociologist Tony Walter, adopts a more positive view of the deceased: "The purpose of grief is not to break the bond with the dead but to integrate the dead into the survivor's ongoing life" (1996). The memories of the dead persist, but we are required to define a new relationship to them. I think of the Mexican Day of the Dead celebrations, when family invite the deceased to return to their homes to be fed and honored, as a good ethnographic example of Walter's interpretation. The dead live on, albeit in a transformed fashion, in traditional Mexican culture.

Reality Check

It always seems to be anthropology's job to show how diverse human behavior is across cultures, and the evidence on grief fits this pattern perfectly. There are many examples of people acting exactly as we would *least* expect them to, as in the case of the Balinese, who seem to laugh at loss as they strive to balance turbulent hearts with the expectations of socially constructed identities (Wikan 1990). In other instances the emotional expression is familiar, but in our eyes it comes from the wrong person. It is not, for example, the widow among the Trobriand Islanders (near New Guinea) who grieves most intensely; it is the deceased's siblings, because in a matrilineal society they are the closest relatives (Weiner 1988). Equally striking are societies whose norms for grief would be treated as pathological by Western culture. The Ifaluk of the Philippines, for instance, once considered it normal for a man who suffered a loss to respond by going on a headhunting expedition, without the ultimate victim necessarily having any connection to the death (Rosaldo 1988). Anger, for the Ifaluk, is the primary emotion of grief.

The idea that six months' time is sufficient for the completion of mourning and alleviation of grief would be laughable to innumerable human communities. Walk through a Spanish or Greek village and notice the widows wearing black, often years after losing a spouse. In traditional Greek culture grief drives the bereaved to unearth and cleanse the bones of the deceased after decomposition has done its work so as to enact a ritual reburial. Even our own culture once granted far more time for societal and individual adjustment to loss, with no thought that prolonged sadness indicated pathology. As recently as the mid-twentieth century it was considered unseemly for a bereaved man or woman even to consider a new relationship for at least a year, not only out of respect for the dead but also because it was assumed the emotions were still too raw, the attachment still too strong.

A clinical social worker sarcastically quipped to me that after two months a widow has yet to figure out how to get the grass cut, much less how to resolve the deep emotions of grief that come in unexpected waves over many months and even years. Confirming this observation, the author Joan Didion, whose words are quoted at the start of this chapter, continued to expect her deceased husband to appear for dinner, to need his shoes, and to be there for smart conversation well into her "year of magical thinking" after his sudden death. The arbitrary demarcation of a time for normal grief is, to my thinking, a questionable application of psychiatric concern.

Grief and the DSM-5

In 1999, just five years after the publication of the Diagnostic and Statistical Manual's fourth edition, the process began for DSM-5. By the time the American Psychiatric Association's Board of Trustees finally approved the new text in December 2012, dozens of work groups, international conferences, study groups, and research reports ("white papers") had contributed to the elaborate process of improving the identification and treatment of mental illnesses (Black and Grant 2014). Through the DSM-5 developmental website, comments were

also solicited from additional professionals and from the public. The resulting 947-page document honored precedents from earlier editions as well as
responded to the controversies and scientific/clinical input that the process
stimulated. Among the changes in the new DSM is a shift in the way grief is
conceived and clinically managed.

In DSM-IV grief appeared as an exclusionary factor for the diagnosis of major
depressive disorder (MDD) on the grounds that symptoms associated with a
significant loss were probably part of normal experience and should, therefore,
not contribute to a diagnosis of MDD. DSM-5 eliminates this exclusion "because
evidence does not support the separation of loss of a loved one from other
stressors in terms of its likelihood of precipitating a major depressive episode"
(American Psychiatric Association 2013, 103). Although most people do not
experience grief at a level of intensity sufficient to trigger serious depression,
for some vulnerable persons it can be so troublesome that they will manifest the
defining symptoms for MDD (e.g., feeling worthless, having suicidal thoughts,
a persistent depressed mood). The fact that a loss precipitated the episode of
MDD should not disqualify the sufferer from the appropriate diagnosis and
treatment. Only clinical judgment can determine whether the normal symptoms
of grief are accompanied by the presence of a major depressive episode (p. 109).

Before this change was adopted, there was a move from some mental health
specialists and researchers to go even further, to add a new diagnostic category
for prolonged grief disorder (PGD), or complicated grief. Prominent among the
proponents of this proposal were Holly G. Prigerson, professor of psychiatry
at Harvard Medical School and director of the Center for Psychosocial Epidemiology and Outcome Research at the Dana Farber Cancer Institute, and
Katherine Shear, professor of psychiatry and project director at the Center for
Complicated Grief at Columbia University. The former, along with a long list of
collaborators, sought to define the diagnostic criteria for PGD through a carefully
designed research project with 291 bereaved individuals who were interviewed
with the Inventory of Complicated Grief three times at discrete intervals after
their loss (Prigerson et al. 2009). The latter, through articles (Shear et al. 2011)
and her center's website (www.complicatedgrief.org), offered critiques of the
DSM-IV bereavement exclusion and argued for a new diagnostic category for
complicated grief.

These efforts, as well as the ultimate DSM-5 modification, generated "unwanted controversy" (American Psychiatric Association 2013, 103). With eye-
catching headlines like "Is Mourning Madness?: The Wrongheaded Movement
to Classify Grief as a Mental Disorder" (Granek and O'Rourke 2012), critics
warned that the changes would make the normal and healthy experience of grief

into a pathology requiring therapy, probably with expensive pharmaceuticals. On the website for the popular magazine *Psychology Today* Allen J. Frances, MD and DSM-IV editor, posted "DSM 5 to the Barricades on Grief: Defending the Indefensible," in which he attacked the "silly and unnecessary proposal to medicalize grief" (Frances 2012). Frances observed that the careful clinical decision making called for in the DSM-5 text related to grief ignores the fact that it is primary care doctors, not psychiatrists, who are responsible for most diagnoses of mental illness and the prescriptions that follow. He warns that the brief time these physicians spend with their patients, their lack of psychiatric training, and the pressure they are under from pharmaceutical representatives will result in "dreadful unintended consequences."

Critics are missing more significant developments by focusing on the elimination of the grief exclusion for the diagnosis of MDD. It isn't just that grief may now be included as a precipitating cause of a major depressive episode; it is also that the DSM-5 authors have opened the door to an eventual addition of a separate diagnosis for complicated grief. This is to be found in two places in the text. First, the paragraph under Depressive Disorders confuses the claim that grief can trigger an MDD with the separate and undefended assertion that persons whose extreme response to grief that contributes to a depressive episode are "at risk for 'complicated grief,' characterized by ruminating about the deceased person, seeking proximity to the deceased person, and striving to avoid experiences that trigger reminders of loss" (American Psychiatric Assocation 2013, 104). By a sleight of hand, the authors have introduced a disease called "complicated grief," which the manual does not yet accept. More than a precipitating factor for MDD, the DSM-5 has created a co-occurring condition called *complicated grief*.

The second place in the text where grief becomes an illness is in a section of the DSM-5 reserved for Conditions for Further Study, but there it goes under the more elaborate name persistent complex bereavement disorder (BCPD) (American Psychiatric Assocation 2013, 473). Although not part of the new canon of accepted diagnoses, this section moves the discussion in that direction and effectively shifts the burden of proof to those who do not want to see a distinction drawn between "normal" and "complicated" grief. It is somewhat reassuring that this set of criteria grants the sufferer a longer period of time before the experiences that are likely common in response to loss become symptoms of PCBD—twelve months instead of the two weeks for MDD—and we can applaud the authors' accommodation to variable "cultural, religious, or age-appropriate norms." However, Frances's concern about primary care physicians' ability to make the subtle clinical distinctions between these criteria would require remains salient.

Grief in an International Context

On a parallel course to the revisions of the DSM, the World Health Organization began the process of updating the International Classification of Diseases (ICD), "the standard diagnostic tool for epidemiology, health management and clinical purposes" used by 117 countries (World Health Organization n.d.). It has a greater scope than the DSM, in that it covers a wider range of health complaints, but the section devoted to Mental and Behavioral Disorders overlaps with the focus of its psychiatric cousin. Like the DSM revision, the ICD-11 will be the product of extensive consultation with many working groups and input from the public via its web-based interface (http://apps.who.int/classifications/icd11/browse/l-m/en).

One of the working groups focuses on Disorders Specifically Associated with Stress. It has more than a dozen members from different countries, including nonspecialists and non-English speakers. Among the proposals it has advanced, based in part on a review of the evidence collected for the DSM-5, is for the creation of a new category, persistent grief disorder (PGD). The defining symptoms are strikingly similar to the DSM disease-in-waiting, persistent complex bereavement disorder, including the stipulation that symptoms must go "far beyond expected social or cultural norms to be diagnosed as PGD" (Maercker and Perkonigg 2013, 561). If approved and added to the final publication, it will give further weight to the movement in the United States to have certain forms of grief treated as a medical condition.

Pathologizing Life's Passages

Critics of biomedicine refer to the "therapeutic restlessness" that leads doctors to expand the scope of their interventions into areas once treated as relatively unproblematic aspects of the human life course. Despite the fact that the vast majority of births—certainly more than 90 percent—would proceed to a successful delivery with no significant medical intrusion, American physicians insist on prenatal testing, fetal monitoring, and, at a completely unjustified rate, caesarean sections.[1] Puberty might once have called for ritual celebrations, but it now demands medication with growth hormones and drugs to focus attention. Menopause was once considered "The Change," a natural shift from fertility to senior status, but it is now an opportunity to treat a "gynecological disorder" with hormonal replacements. We have already noted the degree to which medicine has co-opted the process of dying, turning it into a technological quagmire of ethical dilemmas.

A case can be made that there is serious resistance in the United States to the medicalization of life's passages, including the management of death and its aftermath. There has been a sustained movement for home births under the care of midwives, women's health advocates have demanded a retreat from hormonal therapies at menopause, and hospice as an alternative to hospital-based dying is on the upswing. That said, the challenges to medicine's control over our lives are largely at the margins and concentrated among wealthier and white communities. In addition, medicine has shown itself capable of co-opting many of the change agendas, for example, by adopting the trappings of "natural birth" within the confines of hospitals and under the direct control of physicians or by creating hospice units in hospitals and making sure patients only end up there when every conceivable intervention has been tried. I understand how some scholars see greater challenges to medicine's power, but I am not convinced we have yet to cross any significant bridges in reclaiming control from health care institutions and pharmaceutical companies.

The effort to treat some forms of grief as a disease must be understood in this broader context of medicine's expanding monopoly over life's passages. Like the woman whose labor progresses more slowly than the medical norm and is therefore considered a candidate for pharmacological and/or surgical intervention, the bereaved person whose grief lasts too long or is too severe earns a psychiatric appointment and a trip to the pharmacy. The threat of serious complications—a dead baby in the former case, a suicide in the latter—justifies medical attention even when the risk is low and the "treatment" may exacerbate the condition it targets. It takes a courageous person to opt out of medical responses when the consequences of refusal are painted in the darkest possible light.

Vested interests are behind the extension of medicine's control into areas of life not previously considered "medical." Natural birth yields lower profits and less specialist prestige than high-tech monitoring and surgical delivery. Pharmaceutical sales swell with each new psychological diagnosis that parents can use to explain their child's poor performance in school or unruly adolescent behavior. Creating armies of grief counselors to treat the unpredictable emotions that accompany loss is also good for the bottom line, as will be the market in medications promoted through "direct to consumer" ads modeled after those for the treatment of depression.

Even if we acknowledge the economic and professional motivations behind the medicalization of life's crises, we still have to wonder why the American public is susceptible to the sell: Why are we so quick to turn to the "experts" to manage some of the more turbulent moments in our lives? In the case of grief, is it really necessary to outsource compassion by hiring counselors to do the hard work of comforting our kin and dearest friends? Why are we so afraid of the emotional roller-coaster that follows loss that we feel compelled to buy therapy from a stranger? Must we accept that sorrow has a timetable and a pharmacological solution? We need to consider in more detail what gets in the way of treating grief as a normal and even healthy response to bereavement, as humans have since the earliest evolutionary stages of our species' development.

Grief and the Service Industry

The splintering of social ties and the diminished community structures that characterize modern American life are often cited as reasons for families to contract for services like child care, rehabilitation after major health crises, and assistance for the elderly. With both members of most couples working full time and with relatives commonly living far apart, families have little opportunity to manage the support roles they once performed. There are exceptions, where extended families still live close to one another or where ethnic and immigrant groups struggle to stay together, but economic pressures and a cultural stress on individuality create for most of us a life of tenuous and temporary social ties. Often parents simply have no relative to turn to when the eight weeks of pregnancy leave come to an end, when someone in the family suffers a serious accident or illness, or when their own parents are no longer able to live independently. In such circumstances it is no surprise that caring becomes a commodity.

Turning the management of grief over to service providers is a logical development given this context. If grief is a disease, then we need not feel responsible for the limited time we have to respond to our suffering relative's sorrow; we can leave that to the professionals. For the person grieving, a medical diagnosis can provide more time off from work than is typically permitted after a death and can legitimate the ongoing impact of loss to an impatient world. For a culture dedicated to drugs, what could be better than antidepressant medications to take the edge off the pain?

Those who promote the application of a disease label to grief admit that a very small percentage of the bereaved, perhaps fewer than 5 percent, have serious difficulty coming to terms with their loss. But the existence of a medical label and insurers who will pay the bills will be an irresistible temptation for an irresponsible expansion of the diagnosis to far more than those who are critically in need of help. Just as we have seen a wanton misuse of other psychiatric diagnoses, like attention deficit disorder, so will complicated grief become the disease du jour, diagnosed for a widening pool of individuals who are actually experiencing the very normal feelings triggered by the death of a loved one.

Grief Management and the Normativity of Death

Earlier I cited Jeffery Kauffman's suggestion that we are unable to handle grief because we have lost the cultural script that once guided us through death and its aftermath, what he calls the "normativity of death." But to say that old norms no longer apply is not the same as saying there are no norms at all. Only in the chaos of a disaster or during the total collapse of societal structures caused by war can we talk about a temporary loss of norms, and even in such extreme circumstances patterned social life quickly reasserts itself. I think Kauffman mistakes changing norms for no norms, but he nevertheless calls our attention to the fact that we do not grieve as we once did.

A hallmark of Western civilization that finds its maximum expression in contemporary America is its excessive focus on the individual. Anthropologists have commented on the cultural model of personal autonomy that prevails in Western societies, in contrast to the highly interdependent view of the person that characterizes most other cultures. Clifford Geertz, among the most influential social scientists of the late twentieth century, differentiated between the "socio-centric and relational" view of the individual in non-Western cultures and the "ego-centric and contractual" model that dominates the Western world. The latter is particularly evident in the rights-based system of bioethics, in which the self-determining individual is fully entitled to choose what may be done to him or her. Visitors from other, less individualistically obsessed cultures—Japan would be a good example—often remark on the degree to which people in the West are treated as though they exist without social ties, free to make decisions with no regard to the interests even of intimates.

This asocial view of the person has helped to transform grief from shared sorrow to individual ailment. Whereas in much of the world "it takes a village" to grieve, in the United States we treat the bereaved as solo sufferers, almost as an embarrassment to the rest of us because they insist on injecting emotions into the calm veneer of social interaction. To the casual "How are you doing?" we do not expect and certainly don't want tears and tales of loss.

There are cases in which grief is not treated exclusively as an individual's responsibility, especially when the loss comes as a result of tragedy. We grant the surviving families of those who died on September 11, 2001, the right to publicly and emotionally mourn every year at the anniversary of the attacks. The spouse of a member of the military who perished in combat has a large support community and a license to grieve for extended periods. Some religions—Judaism is a good example—provide both an extended script for mourning and a ready social network to console the bereaved. Hospitals sometimes provide ongoing support services for parents who lose young children, often including annual candlelight services with ritual recitations of the names of the deceased. As the expression has it, grief shared is grief relieved.

These exceptions notwithstanding, most bereaved in America sense that self-help is the expected response to grief. A trip to your local bookstore or an Internet search will supply the resources you need for an efficient and time-sensitive program for recovery. Titles include *The Grief Recovery Handbook, I Wasn't Ready to Say Goodbye Workbook, How to Go On Living When Someone You Love Dies,* and the *Grief Counseling Homework Planner.* And yes, there is also a *Grieving for Dummies.* These useful texts share the bookstore section with weight loss and exercise books. And if they don't work, there's a diagnosis and medications waiting.

When the funeral or memorial service ends, Americans are left to sort out this grief issue largely on their own. It's "pull yourself up by your own bootstraps" applied to mourning. This is the "new normativity" that has come to complicate grief in the West. It is perfectly in sync with the pervasive emphasis on individuality that characterizes so much of American culture, even if it falls short of providing comfort and solace to those in pain. I think the move toward the medicalization of grief is a measure of how poorly our focus on the individual self serves us when we face the loss of a loved one; in the absence of collective support and understanding, we have no choice but to retreat to the white coats and pills that sanction our suffering.

An Alternative Path?

It is probably too much to expect that we will reverse course and rediscover our heritage of more collective responses to grief. But it might be possible to swim against the riptide of individuality by rejecting the pull toward a fully medicalized and desocialized response to sorrow. It isn't too much to ask that we give greater recognition to the hard facts that loss from death hurts, sadness lasts, and, with the support of those who care for us, suffering eventually fades and life goes on. We can be noncompliant when our well-intentioned friends and family urge us to make an appointment with a counselor and instead ask that they listen and be patient. Even if we find comfort in an "expert's" attention, we can still refuse the prescription for an antidepressant, which, in any case, evidence suggests won't work to relieve grief.

I do not mean to suggest that there is no benefit to counseling after experiencing a death. Emotional issues, some not even related directly to the deceased, may arise in the aftermath of loss, and a professional may help the bereaved sort out what he/she is feeling. There are also individuals who may profit from the distance provided by a neutral party, such as a hospice counselor, someone trained to listen for the hidden content behind suffering. Family dynamics may actually exacerbate the bereaved's response to death, whereas a trained expert can provide a relationship of trust and openness that may facilitate coping. But this can all occur without a medical label and, I suspect, without immediate recourse to medications.

Let's be clear: grief *is* complicated, but not necessarily in the medical sense. Though we would like to imagine that our identity is independent of those around us, that we are autonomous actors on life's stage, there are moments in life that demand we pay attention to the pieces of ourselves that have grown through our connections to others. When those others die, we lose a part of our selves, and that will always be painful. There should be no talk of timetables or unacceptable emotional expressions; we must acknowledge that life and loss go together, that grief is not something you just get over like the common cold. We should pay attention to traditions of mourning in which the bereaved are supported by loving family and friends who simply listen without judgment or expectations and who help with the practicalities that accompany death.

How likely it is that this more social and therapeutic approach to grief will reverse the momentum favoring medical intervention? I'm not sure. On the one hand, there are many communities in the United States that still honor a collective response to grief. A particularly striking example is the history of African American funerals and their shared sorrow, especially for victims of unspeakable acts of violence (Holloway 2002). Many Asian American traditions equally affirm kin networks and grief responsibilities defined by age and gender. The traditional Irish American wake is nothing if not a highly social response to grief.

On the other hand, the culture of biomedicine, including psychiatry, is perpetually hungry for new domains to claim for itself, and the pharmaceutical industry is only too willing to promote the expansion of "disease" into unclaimed territory. The fact that both the DSM-5 and, in all likelihood, the ICD-11 are poised to embrace the concept of complicated grief suggests to me that opponents are probably on the losing end of medical history. I can already envision the advertisement for "GriefRelief," a prescription drug that takes the pain out of loss: I see an animated figure bent over a tombstone in near darkness, an ominous voice describing the terrible pain of bereavement, followed by a bright sunrise with a crescendo of happy music and the trademark pill represented as a smiley-faced balloon rising into the blue sky. Then comes the list of potential side effects and the warning that the drug may have no effect on your sorrow. When I'm feeling pessimistic, that's the future I envision.

Chapter 6

Inconvenient Bodies

Dig Unearths Early Black Burial Ground

Churning through the stillness of centuries, a trowel-by-trowel probe has yielded one of the oldest remnants of a black community in New York City—a colonial-era cemetery that was then at the most desolate edge of town and is now 20 feet below the civic center. Thirteen bodies have already been exhumed by archeologists at a construction site at Broadway and Reade Street. It seems certain they are unearthing the "Negros [sic] Burial Ground," documented as early as 1755, which also served as a potter's field and as a graveyard for American prisoners during the Revolutionary War. (Dunlap 1991)

Bad Blood at the Burial Ground

The General Services Administration, the Federal agency responsible for the construction of a courthouse and office building at the site . . . told the city that it would be too expensive to stop construction. According to the Government, $30 million would be squandered if work were halted. But how do you place a price on history? Is the record of our earliest African residents—people who helped build colonial New York, laid the cobblestones of our first streets and fought in the Revolution—worth $30 million? The agency's response caused an uproar. Finally, after a threatened protest and a Congressional hearing, it promised that work would stop until the Government presented the city with an acceptable plan. (Macdonald 1992)

Mortal Dilemmas: The Troubled Landscape of Death in America, by Donald Joralemon, 95–108. © 2016 Left Coast Press, Inc. All rights reserved.

Wherein lies the power of human remains? How is it that the bones of 419 free and enslaved Africans interred in lower Manhattan between 1690 and 1790 were resurrected to great fanfare four hundred years later? Their accidental discovery halted a massive federal construction project. They were scientifically sampled and studied by scholars at Howard University and then ceremoniously re-interred at a newly created national memorial erected at the site of their original burial. Dignitaries from the political and arts worlds spoke at the ritual; a Yoruba priest added African blessings and prayers as the coffins were lowered back into the ground. How did the bones of those who were powerless in life come to demand such reverence in death?

We invoke the ethic of respect for bodies, whatever their state of decomposition, when the interests of the living threaten the peace of the deceased. Yet a strong current of thought in America attributes no ongoing identity to the material remains of the dead. For example, cremation, which has grown in popularity over the past decades, depends on a strictly material view of the corpse. In the medical world cadavers in anatomy labs are treated as teaching tools devoid of personhood, although the detachment of body from self is not always easy for students to embrace. Organ transplantation also depends on the separation of person from body, despite ambivalence from both donor families and recipients about whether the deceased lives on in his/her relocated organs.

The view that self survives in corporeal remains is also strong, as the reburial described above demonstrates. Relatives of those killed in natural and human-made disasters passionately pursue the recovery of even a small fragment of their loved ones' bodies, as that biological particle is thought to carry some part of the individual's identity. Surviving family members from the 2001 World Trade Center attacks struggled to have tons of rubble sifted and searched for any human remains and insisted that sophisticated genetic testing be done to link even the smallest piece to a specific individual. The same insistence on recovery and return of remains follows natural catastrophes such as earthquakes and hurricanes. The huge investment of time and money in these activities is only sensible if the living feel a continuing attachment to the material leftovers from life. That attachment must be built on the idea that something of the person remains in the corpse.

We will be in a better position to understand the commitment to cadavers in America after looking at some particularly interesting examples of bodies that were either intentionally or unintentionally unearthed. We start with an example of intentional exhumation and relocation and then return to cases like the African American graveyard in Manhattan, where graves were accidentally uncovered during building projects. Finally, we'll consider a category of disturbed remains that has special legal standing in the United States thanks to the Native American Grave and Repatriation Act (1990). The key questions will be: Which bodies matter, why, to whom, and for how long? The overarching ethical issue is: What limits, if any, apply to the principle that we should respect human remains, and what does "respect" entail?

Colma: Where the Dead Outnumber the Living

The Bay Area Rapid Transit train leaves you off one block from the seventeen cemeteries that make up the "San Francisco Necropolis" in Colma, California. Nestled between highways, shopping malls, and suburban neighborhoods are the dead of the city by the bay. The earliest residents, beginning to occupy the Holy Cross Cemetery in 1887, were relocated from graveyards within San Francisco's city limits, evicted when the value of property made it economically inconvenient to allow the deceased to compete for space with the living. The push for relocation was given added impetus when San Francisco newspapers, public health officials, and politicians began to warn that the "invisible effluvia that rise in the air from the cities of the dead contain gaseous poisons of the most deadly character" (Svanevik and Burgett 1995). When officials had notified as many living kin as could be found of their ancestors' pending move, they grouped the rest into large communal burials in the new setting. At the time Colma was farmland, with sufficient open space to accommodate a growing population of dead residents.

Even in death nationality and religious background matter. A large sign above the main road, El Camino Real, announces the Italian Cemetery (see Figure 6.1). Across the street is the final resting place for Greek Orthodox bodies. There's ground reserved for Jews, Roman Catholics, Serbians, Japanese, and Chinese. And then there is the hillside "Pets' Rest" where, since 1947, dogs, cats, and some more exotic animal companions—an ocelot, a horse, and an iguana—have been buried by their human families with appropriately designed tombstones (e.g., in the shape of a dog bone) and clever epitaphs, such as "Life with Tweeter couldn't be sweeter."

Eventually the newly dead joined the ranks of the relocated. Elaborate interments for some of San Francisco's most elite citizens were facilitated by a spur of the Southern Pacific Railroad with specially equipped funeral cars like El Descanso ("The Rest"). Among the more famous of Colma's estimated 1.5 million dead are Levi Strauss, Wyatt Earp, and Joe DiMaggio. Notable architects vied for commissions to design impressive family mausoleums, many inspired

Figure 6.1
One of seventeen cemeteries in Colma, California.
Courtesy of Donald Joralemon.

by Egyptian and Neoclassical styles. At one time there were twenty monument companies within the city limits and just as many flower shops.

It takes a village of workers to keep the grass cut, the decaying flowers removed, and the numerous fountains running. I asked a Mexican American worker at one cemetery whether it bothered him to be working with his weed wacker around so many dead people. He said, "No, they don't mind. I'm keeping their neighborhood clean." The historical museum for the cemeteries is just down the street from the Lucky Chance Casino, a revenue source for a town that can't collect taxes from the dead. An elderly gentleman was glad to show me the memorabilia from a century's worth of the burial business. The gift shop offers a bumper sticker that reads "It's great to be alive in Colma."

San Francisco was not the only American city to relocate its dead when they threatened development. In 1850 Chicago moved cemeteries occupying valuable land along the river and lake fronts, only to have to repeat the process fifty years later as the expanding city encroached on the second site. St. Louis authorities seemed not to have noticed when highway construction workers plowed aside sections of Washington Park Cemetery in the 1950s, but when plans in the 1990s for the MetroLink light rail system near Lambert International Airport called for a route right through the same cemetery, twenty-eight hundred graves were respectfully relocated. This work delayed construction by nearly a year and added some $2 million to the project's cost.

Engineers working for the New Jersey Turnpike Authority used ground-penetrating radar in 2001 to establish the boundaries of a graveyard that stood in the way of a highway interchange. Some nine hundred bodies, many from local health institutions serving the poor and mentally ill, had to be exhumed and relocated at an estimated cost of $1 million. This devotion to the dead is somewhat unusual in comparative and historical terms. In Medieval Europe it was customary to unearth bodies to make room for new residents, the bones being stored in passageways and rooms beneath churches or in specially constructed charnel houses. Overcrowding in cemeteries in Victorian England was resolved by burning remains after twelve years. In contemporary times families lease graves for established periods—fifty years in Berlin, fifteen in Denmark—on the assumption that fresh corpses should take the space from those that have been reduced to skeletons. In many countries some variety of communal burial is the destination for bones once stripped of flesh.

Yet the reuse of burial plots after sufficient time has passed for complete decomposition seems anathema to American sensibilities. National headlines on July 8, 2009, reported the arrest of four workers at the Burr Oak Cemetery near Alsip, Illinois. They were accused of having resold hundreds of burial plots after unearthing and dumping the original inhabitants elsewhere on the 150-acre memorial park. The alleged conspirators were charged with *dismembering a human body*, a felony that carries up to thirty years in prison. Over twenty FBI agents and two forensic anthropologists assisted in the investigation that followed the arrests. What was treated as a "cemetery nightmare" in the United States would have been conventional practice in many other societies, where "human body" and "skeletal remains" are different moral categories.

We may have to reconsider the sanctity of cemeteries as places for the dead to rest for eternity. At this point in history about 2.5 million people die in the United States every year. Although just over a third of those deaths are followed by cremation, that still leaves nearly nine hundred thousand bodies to bury annually. An average grave site measures two and a half by eight feet, or 20 square feet. Multiply the number of dead to be buried by the size of the graves they will occupy, and it is clear that much more space, mostly in already densely populated areas, will be required to inter so many new bodies. We may have to develop a recycling approach to cemetery plots or expand on the tradition of mausoleums with vertical stacking. America is a large country, but isn't that a lot of real estate to reserve for the dead?

Neglected Graves, Accidental Discovery

Far more common than the neatly tended cemeteries of Colma are those that no one visits. They may be too small to draw attention, or as the years pass and descendants move away, there may be no one left to tend the graves. They are often the resting grounds of people considered unimportant, not worth the sort of monuments that persist through time. Their headstones or simple wooden markers fall, decay, and are overgrown. Town archives may not record their existence.

Road projects, housing developments, and the construction of dams are plotted on maps that may not testify to the presence of these dead. But when a bucket load of bones drops before the startled tractor operator, a moment of decision arrives: proceed with the work and deliver the remains to a landfill without notice, or call the authorities. The choice is influenced as much by legal codes as moral principles. In some states the penalties are severe if anyone, perhaps a nosey reporter, discovers that graves have been disturbed and skeletons discarded with the trash. But construction delays are expensive, and there is no love lost between contractors and the historians and archaeologists who may insist on time to investigate and document.

The construction of the Superdome complex in New Orleans during the late 1960s and early 1970s unearthed a nineteenth-century cemetery. This caused no concern until fill from the site was sold to area homeowners and the valuable topsoil was found to include skeletal material. Residents worried that they might be exposed to posthumous germs. It is noteworthy that disease, not burial disturbance, was the issue for local citizens. No one seems to have clamored for a respectful reburial.

A very different response to old bones came during an Army Corps of Engineers project along the Red River in southwest Arkansas in 1980. When workers uncovered a tombstone and partial skeleton, a call was placed to the Arkansas Archaeological Survey, with the result that the site was determined to include both historical and prehistoric graves. Construction stopped and scientific excavations began. A total of 125 historical graves were documented, but questions remained about what to do with them. The National Registry of Historic Places will only consider a cemetery for protection if it "derives its primary significance from graves of persons of transcendent importance from age, from distinctive design features, or from association with historic events" ("National Register Criteria for Evaluation" n.d.). Legal opinions were solicited and local officials consulted. The solution was to accept an offer from the Elders of the Cedar Grove Baptist Church for reburial, after scientific observations were completed, on land deeded to the church. New boxes with metal inventory tags accommodated the bones, and a large communal tombstone marked the new site. It took well over a year to settle all the legal and practical issues associated with this accidental discovery.

The value of bones in this case, as with the African American remains found in Manhattan, was explicitly tied to what they could reveal about the past after scientific analysis. A letter from Carol Schull, an official at the National Registry, to Colonel Sands of the New Orleans District of the Army Corps (May 28, 1981) clarified that cemeteries are eligible for protection if they "may yield information important in the understanding of broad patterns of our history" (Limp and Rose 1986). Given this priority, it is not surprising that the website for the African Burial Ground National Monument in New York (www.africanburial-ground.gov) links to three "technical reports" based on scientific and historical investigations of the cemetery and its human remains: the African Burial Ground Final History Report, the African Burial Ground Final Skeletal Biology Report, and the African Burial Ground Final Archaeology Report.

The scientific promise of bones has not always led to an expeditious and respectful reburial after analysis. For example, the Smithsonian Institution once possessed some thirty-three thousand human skeletons, most of which collected dust in the museum's storage rooms without any attention from scholars. These bones crossed a conceptual boundary between human remains and human *artifacts*, the latter category being subject to the peculiar logic of collecting for the pure sake of collecting. That the material might be valuable to some researcher at some future time is the curator's justification for shelf after shelf of boxed bodies. Not everyone accepts that science trumps respect for the dead.

Bones as Collectables

Dr. C. Edward Hitchcock (1828–1911) was a professor of hygiene and physical education at Amherst College. Across the valley, at Smith College, Professor Harris Hawthorne Wilder (1864–1928) taught zoology. The two scientists found they had a common interest: collecting human and material artifacts from Native American graves in the vicinity of their respective institutions. Local farmers knew to notify them when plows unearthed bones or other Indian cultural material, but Hitchcock and Wilder also organized weekend excavations with family and students to known Indian settlements, sometimes in search of the burials of specific native leaders. Mrs. Hitchcock, who assisted her husband on these digs, remarked that their "kitchen was being constantly requisitioned for boiling out skeletons" (Loomis 1915).[1]

For these two men it was not bones for bones sake alone. They measured and recorded what they collected as an exercise in what they considered a scholarly investigation. They embraced the fledgling science of anthropometry, which asserted a direct correlation between physical features—especially cranial size—and race-based intelligence. Native Americans, or "savages" as Hitchcock called them, were thought to be primitive, uncivilized, and of a lower intelligence than their white conquerors. Their physical remains would provide evidence of their mental limitations, or so thought these nineteenth-century scientists.

Hitchcock and Wilder gave their collections homes at their respective institutions, the former in the Gilbert Collection under the supervision of Amherst's Geology Department and the latter in the Smith Anthropological and Zoological Museum, a rather grand name for a basement storage room. There the bones and artifacts rested, rarely used once anthropometry's racist speculations were refuted.

It was not just these two academics who found that Indian bones and artifacts were worthy collectables; professional archaeologists and amateur hobbyists put trowels to work across the country in both large- and small-scale excavations. Some of the material made its way into museums and historical societies, but much more remained in private hands to be traded and sold in ever-expanding informal and formal markets. Few questioned ownership rights or challenged the ethics of disturbing Indian graves—that is, until Native Americans joined forces in the last decades of the twentieth century to demand legal rights and cultural respect.

One outcome of the American Indian Movement in the United States was the adoption by Congress of the Native American Grave Protection and Repatriation Act (NAGPRA) in 1990. Any museum or other institution receiving federal funds would be obligated to inventory Native American remains, artifacts found in association with graves, and objects of "cultural patrimony" in their collections. Whenever "cultural affiliation"[2] with current recognized tribes could be established, the law required notification of tribal representatives to determine what would be done with the artifacts. Tribes were legally authorized to demand transfer, or "repatriation," for whatever purpose they considered proper. In the case of human remains, this often meant ceremonial reburial.

The anthropologist Marge Bruchac wrote her doctoral thesis on the history of the Hitchcock and Wilder collections, including the efforts of Smith and

Amherst Colleges and the University of Massachusetts at Amherst to comply with NAGPRA regulations. (Bruchac 2007). She was in a unique position to do this research, being herself of Native American ancestry (Abenaki), a graduate of Smith College, and an anthropology graduate student at the University of Massachusetts. Her background was even more perfectly suited to the task set for her as research liaison to the Five College[3] Repatriation Committee, which I briefly chaired. The committee's mission was to expedite the inventory of Native American material held at the colleges and the university and to facilitate the repatriation process. Marge helped forge a productive relationship with the Native American groups whose ancestors were likely included in the collections; it was her suggestion that tribal representatives be brought into the process early on to give them the opportunity to provide guidance in the respectful treatment of the remains. She also pioneered a novel methodology to identify the probable origins of excavated material and to assist a professional osteologist in the oftentimes difficult process of reassembling skeletons with parts that had been traded and exchanged within the network of collectors.

Soon after we began our work, in September of 2003, Marge made the arrangements for an initial gathering of tribal representatives and the committee. Our Native American guests, from six tribal groups, met first with each other and then with us all together. What can be a tense relationship between academics and tribal authorities over NAGPRA-sensitive material was, in this case, a powerful lesson in the meaning of bones. As Marge put it in a report on the conference, "Native remains and artifacts in the local colleges are now being recognized, not just as curious dead objects owned by institutions, but as living collections, incorporating remains of the ancestors, and artifacts with intrinsic sacred value and legal status."

The key to a successful interaction between academics and Native Americans in this instance was that the former made no proprietary claim based on the scientific merits of the skeletons unearthed by Hitchcock and Wilder. Likewise, the tribal representatives were willing to accept that some scientific investigation was critical to the proper identification of cultural affiliation and skeletal reconstruction. The Hitchcock and Wilder archives had to be mined for information about where and when they excavated as well as how they exchanged material—a cranium for stone implements, for example. A professional bone specialist was needed to attempt the reunification of individuals' skeletal parts. A working balance was achieved between the priorities of academic analysis and ancestral return. This has not always been the case with Native American remains.

Who Owns the Bones?

The cities of Kennewick, Pasco, and Richland in southeast Washington have hosted annual hydroplane boat races on the Columbia River for over forty years. This late-July weekend event attracts spectators from all over the state and country. Local residents Will Thomas and Dave Deacy were at the river's edge in 1996, waiting for the final race. Will was wading about ten feet offshore when his foot hit a round object that turned out to be a human skull. The two hid the skull in some bushes along the bank, watched the last race, and then returned with a bucket. They turned the find over to the Kennewick police, who went to the site and found more bones along the shore, apparently from the same individual. They cordoned the area off as a potential crime scene.

The local coroner asked forensic anthropologist James C. Chatters to study the bones. Chatters initially suspected they were the remains of a European settler but revised that judgment when, within a month, the results of a CT scan and radiocarbon dating indicated much greater antiquity, between 7300 and 7600 BC. Even more intriguing, Charters thought the physical character- istics of the skull were inconsistent with current Native Americans, suggesting to him that the skeleton might challenge existing ideas about the migration of populations from Asia to North America. Chatters quickly concluded that "Kennewick Man," as the skeleton was soon named, could provide invaluable insights into the early history of humans in the Western Hemisphere.

It was unfortunate that Chatters chose to characterize the skull as "Cauca- soid" because that almost immediately generated sensational media reports about "white" settlers of the "New World" that predated Amerindians. As the anthropologist Fernando Armstrong-Fumero (2014) points out, this situation was further exacerbated when an artist's model based on the skull was com- pared by Chatters to the actor Patrick Stewart, an English actor who played Captain Jean-Luc Picard in the television series *Star Trek: The Next Generation*. That was enough for some fringe groups to co-opt the Kennewick story for their own purposes. A Neo-Nazi Internet forum, *Stormfront*, used the resem- blance to promote the idea that "Aryans" had been in the Western Hemisphere well before Columbus's voyage. Among the parties that came forward to claim rights to the skeleton was the Asatru Folk Assembly, a religious group founded in 1994 with the goal of promoting the "survival and welfare of the Northern European peoples as a cultural and biological group" (http://asatrufolkassembly .org/about-the-afa/declaration-of-purpose/).

Just days after the radiocarbon dates came back, the Army Corps of Engineers took possession of the skeleton on the grounds that the discovery site was on land it controls. The Corps immediately filed a NAGPRA notice of "intent to repatriate" to an alliance of five tribes and bands: the Umatilla, Yakama, Nez Perce, Wanapum, and Colville. Native representatives made it clear that they would not permit further study of the bones; they intended to rebury them in a secret location. Despite numerous requests from citizens, scientists, and politicians to allow additional analysis, the Corps proceeded with the planned repatriation, even allowing tribal representatives into a "secure storage site" to remove several of the bones for burial.

A legal battle ensued when eight anthropologists, including two from the Smithsonian Institution, filed suit to stop the Corps from turning the skeleton over to the Native American groups. They made two arguments. First, the NAGPRA requirement that "cultural affiliation" between the remains and con-temporary Native American groups had not been established and, thus, the Act did not apply. Second, "repatriation will deprive scholars of any opportunity or right to study this treasure. . . . Study of the skeleton would be of a major benefit to the United States."[4] In essence the anthropologists were arguing that based on the initial study, Kennewick man was not an ancestor of any of the groups demanding ownership under NAGPRA, and even if that affiliation could be demonstrated, the greater good of scientific knowledge outweighed tribal respect for the dead.

This was a battle the Army Corps was not interested in fighting, so they turned jurisdiction over to the Department of the Interior (DOI) in March of 1998. The DOI reviewed the case and, in 2000, decided that by the "prepon-derance of the evidence [the bones] are culturally affiliated with the present-day Indian tribe claimants." The anthropologists immediately amended their complaint in response to the DOI finding. In August 2002 Federal Judge John Jelderks, after reviewing the twenty-two-thousand-page administrative report from the DOI, decided in favor of the scientists and ordered that the skeleton be made available for additional study. The 9th US Circuit Court of Appeals upheld the lower court's decision in February of 2004, and the scientists finally had the green light to investigate further, fully eight years after Will Thomas stubbed his toe on a half-submerged skull.

Native Americans who assign sacred significance to their ancestral bones face a difficult catch-22 under NAGPRA rules. The requirement that cultural affilia-tion must be demonstrated before NAGPRA applies opens the door to precisely the sort of scientific analysis that some tribes consider an offense against their forbearers, but without that evidence the bones lack the act's protections against disrespectful use. Even more complicated, some Native American representatives reject the authority of scientific inquiry altogether. One spokesperson, when confronted with the argument that Kennewick Man, or the "Ancient One" as the skeleton was known by native groups, could reveal much about the early migrations into the Western Hemisphere, said, "We already know our history. It is passed on to us through our elders and through our religious practices." In short, "we" don't need your science to tell us where we came from.

Scientists are also frustrated by the impediments NAGPRA places in the way of investigations they view as critical to a full understanding of human history. They find it unacceptable that the act validates evidence of cultural affiliation that comes from "folklore, oral tradition, historical, or other relevant information or expert opinion" and that it permits "gaps" in the lines connecting remains to current populations. Scientists react against the dismissal of their evidence as secondary to sacred myths and origin stories. They argue that bones of sufficient antiquity, like Kennewick Man/Ancient One, belong to all of humanity and have primary value for the insights they can offer about our past.

There is an important international context to the repatriation debate that unfolded in Washington State. The Altai Princess, or Ice Maiden, found on the Ukok plateau of Russia stimulated a similar dispute between science and indigenous activists, as did the Lake Mungo Burials in Australia. In a comparative analysis of the three cases, the Belgian archaeologist Gertjan Plets (2014, 76) and his coauthors offer this useful conclusion:

> Something from the past is not a heritage object just because it is from the past; heritage is not self-defining but the result of a social action of meaning making. . . . An object becomes heritage when people attach values to it and use it for their own agendas. These values are not universal but individually held, context-dependent, and a reflection of what groups of people appraise or repudiate in the present or future.

For all the conflicts engendered by the application of NAGPRA regulations in the United States, there has been a net positive for the field of archaeology. Consistent with our experience in the Five Colleges of Western Massachusetts, there is a new openness to the recognition that the perceived scientific value of bones has to be reconciled with the meanings associated with human remains as critical parts of a people's heritage. "NAGPRA and especially Kennewick promoted a new archeological practice whereby intercultural and consultations became central; alternative archaeologies also received more attention" (Plets et al. 2014, 86).[5]

Conclusion

The meaning of bones is clearly unsettled and contentious. For many the individuality of human remains diminishes as they go from "wet" to "dry," from flesh and tissue to skeletal material. For others the spirit of the deceased cannot rest if its remains are disturbed, no matter how thoroughly decomposed they may be. By this view a nine-thousand-year-old skull and its associated bones deserve a respectful disposition, even were it originally buried by the accidental processes of nature rather than the intentional labor of friends and family.

We learn from examples of disrupted burials that the significance of the dead is entirely dependent on who, if anyone, has a stake in the deceased's "eternal rest." In a highly mobile and atomistic society like the United States, where the most significant family relations are typically restricted to the nuclear family, there is likely to be a small pool of persons with an emotional stake in grave protection, and that group will probably diminish rapidly as generations pass and descendants relocate. For groups like Native Americans, with a strong sense of common identity expressed through clan and tribal affiliations, the number of persons who experience a connection to the dead will be much larger. Add to that a worldview that affirms a continuing tie between living and dead, and the passage of time will probably not reduce the commitment to caring for bones.

It is not just the size and significance of kin groups that may affect the attachment felt to interred remains; as we saw in the case of Colma, a shared immigration history and/or religious identity can create bonds to the remains even of strangers. Military service and work in some professions (e.g., police and firemen) also provide ready-made constituencies who will care about the graves of comrades they may never have known. Deaths that result from large-scale disasters—natural or human caused—can stimulate a commemorative impulse that spans social groups and persists through time. The deaths of notable figures, from politicians to artists, similarly guarantee the long-term protection of burials.

We can return to the question that opened this chapter: What exactly do people respect when human remains are treated with reverence? Perhaps the better question is what is left of the person to be respected when a living body has been subject to the decay and decomposition that follow death? The deceptively obvious answer is memory, either of the person once associated with those body parts or of some aspect of the person with which the living are still concerned (e.g., his/her historical role, ethnicity, occupational affiliation). It is memory that demands respect, not the material residue of a life long ago lost. And yet memory and materiality are not easily separated from one another.

For some people and some cultures the material remains of a human life provide a bridge to memories of the deceased. They are inanimate objects that are animated—or, should I say, reanimated—by their capacity to provoke a recall of the past, to bring back to life the experiences and emotions that the living once shared with the departed. In this sense bodily remains are memorabilia not unlike photo albums and treasured possessions; they are respected largely because we fear losing the connection they offer to a part of our own past. Respecting human remains is an oddly selfish act.

There is more to the story of human remains. The next chapter explores the creation of death memorials, monuments to individuals and groups whose deaths require more than a simple grave and fitting epitaph. Has America taken memorials a bit too far? Are the roadside altars, commemorative statues, and architectural tributes indications of an obsession to memory?

Chapter 7

Remember

Leverett Neighborhood Wrestles with Weight of a Cross

When Phyllis Glazier sits down to watch TV in her living room, she can see through her window a small wooden cross on the other side of North Leverett Road. The cross commemorates a one-car accident that took place there at 2 a.m. on May 8, 2002, in which 12-year-old Sean Snow died. Two of the Glaziers' neighbors have asked that the cross be removed, but she disagrees with them.

"Whatever makes the bereaved parents feel better is what those who live around it should accept," she said. "It's a terrible thing to lose a child."

The cross was made by Mark Snow of Shutesbury, the boy's father. It features carved letters spelling out "Sean Snow." A photograph of Sean and the words "In loving memory" and "I'm missing you" are on the cross. ("Leverett Neighborhood Wrestles with Weight of a Cross" 2008)

On the first day of my course on dying and death I announced a homework assignment: find death in your immediate environment. When the class next met, the students had found "death everywhere on this campus." One remarked that "there are more memorials here than in a graveyard. Even the trees have somebody's name attached to them." Others pointed out that buildings, classrooms, and books in the library were given in someone's memory. Death was everywhere.

Some cultures strive to forget the dead. The Wari' of Brazil's Amazon, whose "compassionate cannibalism" (Conklin 2001) I described in Chapter

Mortal Dilemmas: The Troubled Landscape of Death in America, by Donald Joralemon, 109–122. © 2016 Left Coast Press, Inc. All rights reserved.

5, dedicated themselves to the obliteration of anything that might recall the deceased to close relatives to speed the dead on their way to the underwater world of the ancestors. The revulsion of the corpse consumers underscored the lengths to which they would go to protect their kin from the terrible effects of a continued attachment to the dead. When missionaries and colonists forced the Wari' to bury rather than ingest their corpses, the community resisted. The thought of a family member rotting in the wet earth was far more troubling than quick and clean consumption. Slow decay promised continued angst for survivors who would retain corporeal memories of loved ones.

Many other societies refuse the dead a continuing presence in the living world by less dramatic customs. Some groups insist that the name of a dead relative never be spoken again. For the Yanomami of Venezuela the mere mention of a dead person's name, much less the display of his/her photograph, can trigger a violent reaction. Conversely, some societies seem to revel in remembrance. Think of the festivities of Mexico's Day of the Dead, when ancestors are seduced back to their homes with altars that feature their favorite foods and drinks and when families congregate in cemeteries in mass celebrations of the fluid line between life and death. The ongoing reverence for ancestors so common in Asian societies is another example of the dead being kept alive by continued ritual acts.

Where does contemporary America stand on the continuum from remembering to forgetting? Some scholars argue that we have become so focused on remembering the dead that we are suffering from "memorial mania," "an obsession with issues of memory and history and an urgent desire to express and claim those issues in visibly public contexts" (Doss 2010, 2). Virtually every town has at least one monument to war casualties, a library or hospital wing with the deceased donor's name attached, schools named after famous deceased figures, and parks that bear the name of a local notable long since buried. Street names honor our ancestors. Roadside memorials, like that dedicated to the memory of Sean Snow in Leverett, Massachusetts, are erected where lives are lost in automobile accidents (Dickinson and Hoffmann 2014).

In our nation's capital the sense of space dedicated to remembering the dead is especially powerful. The most famous presidents get impressive monuments, every national conflict gets extensive treatment with statues and substantial architectural constructions, and an immense and somber graveyard conceived as our "national cemetery" lies just over the Potomac River. The halls of Congress are filled with portraits and marble busts of significant political leaders of the past. A museum pays tribute to the victims of the Nazi holocaust. As my students said, death is everywhere.

Let's take a look at this cultural predilection to memorialize, with an eye to the way other cultures have responded to the management of collective memory. Memorials can be structures or monuments, large or small, but they can also be transitory rituals through which friends and family commemorate a dead person's life. What is certain is that America has pushed the envelope when it comes to remembering.

Body as Memorial

In ancient Peru, when the lord of the Inca Empire died, his kin wrapped his treated body into a large decorated bundle and kept it ready for public display at major festivals, not as a deceased relic but as a still-living force. His relatives had good reason to want his memory preserved and his death reconfigured as eternal life, as it was through him that they were entitled to all the privileges that accompanied his status as the "son of the sun god." Collective self-interest motivated the kin group to deny death and to incorporate the deceased into the living community.

Something of the same logic must have led the political elite of Russia to mummify Vladimir Lenin upon his death in 1924 and put him in a grand mausoleum in the center of Red Square in the capital city, Moscow. The laboratory charged with preserving the body at first employed just four scientists, but by 1945 thirty-five experts toiled against the forces of decay: histologists, anatomists, biochemists, physical chemists, and opticians (Zbarsky and Hutchinson 1998). The mixture of terror and awe that his subjects felt when he ruled was perpetuated by the impression of immortality that accompanies an unchanging corpse; loyal citizens who visited the mausoleum left with a sense that the great leader might just arise from his long slumber and once again take up the reins of power. Subsequent Russian rulers tap into Lenin's aura of invincibility by standing atop the mausoleum to review massive military parades. The chairman is dead; long live the chairman!

Modern America offers an odd innovation on the theme of the preserved corpse as a "living" memorial. A thirty-nine-year-old Texas death-row inmate, Joseph Paul Jernigan, gained a kind of digital immortality when he agreed to donate his body to the Visible Human Project. After prison officials ended his life with a lethal injection, his corpse was frozen, cut into fourths and then sliced into 1,878 one-millimeter-thick sections, which were then digitally photographed and made available to students, researchers, and the curious public at a website maintained by the National Library of Medicine. Joseph's digital self was renamed "Adam" and was soon joined in the ether by "Eve," a fifty-nine-year-old woman who agreed to an anonymous donation in anticipation of her death by heart disease. Eve was sectioned into 5,189 slices. Both residents of this Internet Eden may be inspected in as many ways as one might wish: intact bodies, skeletal structure, organ systems, and cellular close-ups. Maybe one day a digital snake, complete with apple, will be added to this electronic family from Genesis.

Then there is the extended cadaver family of Dr. Gunther von Hagens, the German anatomist who pioneered a technique he calls "plastination" to preserve bodies. After embalming and dehydration, the corpse's tissues are infused with liquid plastics that stop decomposition and produce a flexible, life-like mummy. Dr. von Hagen has taken the "stiff" out of the dead body and thereby created an opportunity for mass exhibitions reminiscent of nineteenth-century carnival freak shows. Posed in every imaginable position, from horseback rider to reclining nude with open abdomen, the good doctor's cadavers have fascinated and perhaps educated over 40 million visitors to Body Worlds, an exhibit of plastinated humans that has opened in over ninety cities in Asia, Africa, Europe, and North America ("The Unparalleled Success" n.d.).[1]

Perhaps these modern cadavers are more anatomy lessons than memorials, bodies apparently stripped of identity, reduced to physical materiality. Looking at a digital slice of Jernigan's pancreas or through the abdomen of von Hagen's reclining nude doesn't demand a memory of the person once associated with those bodies. But the borderline revulsion these immortalized remains inspire must ultimately be due to our tendency to see the person in the cadaver, even when it has been sliced and diced or transformed into life-sized, anatomically correct plastic dolls. It may be humankind rather than a particular human that is being memorialized, but the spectator is still asked to remember the life behind the digital image and synthetic flesh.

Objects and Monuments to Remember By

Mementos of the dead come in every size, shape, and form: a locket holds a strand of the deceased's hair, a photograph freezes moments in a past life, a favorite article of clothing seems to hold a person's essence, or a personal journal or memoir records one's significant experiences for future generations. We've abandoned the European custom from earlier centuries of turning body parts—especially those of religious figures—into mementos or "relics" to be enshrined in pilgrimage spots. The Church of the Holy Cross in Jerusalem, for example, claims to have the finger bone of St. Thomas the Apostle, from the same finger he used to determine whether the wounds on the body of Jesus Christ were real. Unfortunately a vestige of the custom of using body parts as mementos persists in the macabre efforts of devotees to secure a part of the remains of secular stars. The burials of celebrities, from Marilyn Monroe to Michael Jackson, must be protected from pathological fans in pursuit of their own personal relic.

The most traditional memorial, an inscribed gravestone, has undergone a technological update in contemporary America. Photographs of the deceased can be digitally engraved into a headstone. For the media sophisticate, a solar-powered video screen with a repeating loop can be inserted into a monument. The Vidstone Serenity Panel "provides families with the option of viewing a custom-created multimedia tribute at a loved one's place of rest. . . . At the mere touch of a button, a five- to eight-minute video plays on the screen, recounting the most precious and poignant memories of a loved one" (www. vidstone.com). Apparently sales have been slow ("Hi-Tech Tombstone Sales Are Slow Going" 2007).

How, where, and by whom the dead are memorialized can be the subject of intense disputes. Vietnam War veterans were vocal opponents of the winning design for a memorial to be sited on the mall in Washington, DC. The successful plan was the work of a young Asian American, Maya Ying Lin, whose ethnicity triggered racist attacks from those veterans who had learned to generalize a hatred for anyone of Asian descent. Worse, the design was unorthodox, not based on the traditions of patriotic soldier statues. Two angled black granite walls, each sloping into the ground to meet well below surface level, would have the names of casualties inscribed in an order that had the first and last to be killed both appear at the center. One critic called it a "black gash of shame," linking the subterranean design to the abuse suffered by veterans when they returned in defeat from an unpopular conflict. President Ronald Reagan's Secretary of the Interior, James Watt, refused to issue the requisite construction permits until agreement was reached for a second, more conventional memorial, the Three Serviceman Statue, to be erected nearby. A third monument, to women who served in Vietnam, was ultimately added for gender balance.

Ironically the controversial "Wall" has become one of the most often-visited monuments in the country's capital; over 25 million people have seen the monument itself and countless more have viewed the replica wall that travels the country. Families and friends trace the names of loved ones and leave all manner of mementos behind. Every day Washington Park rangers collect the items and add them to the Vietnam Veterans Memorial Collection. Among the over fifty thousand artifacts are photographs, letters, MIA/POW bracelets, medals, helmets, dog tags, boots, canned food, unopened beer cans, cigarettes, birthday cards, toys, bullets, and casings (http://www.nps.gov/americasbestidea/templates/conserving_artifacts.html). Representative samples from the collection have been on exhibit at the Smithsonian Institution.

Controversy also plagued plans for a memorial to those who were killed in the terrorist attacks on the World Trade Center on September 11, 2001. Some considered the entire site to be sacred, a de facto cemetery for the nearly three thousand who died there that day. City and state officials were committed to a plan that would balance the redevelopment of a business center with a space to commemorate the dead. The compromise set aside as a memorial a small part of the space made vacant by debris removal. An international design competition in 2003 yielded 5,200 proposals (1,421 were submitted for the Vietnam War Memorial). The winning plan, titled "Reflecting Absence," transforms the original footprints of the two towers into two deep pools with waterfalls cascading down the side walls. The pools have a surrounding bronze parapet into which are engraved the names of the victims of the attack (see Figure 7.1). A contemplative plaza with symbolically selected trees surrounds the pools, and a separately designed museum houses artifacts from the wreckage, including the famous "Survivors' Stairs," one of the few structural elements left standing after the buildings collapsed. The exhibit space is deep underground, at the level of the bedrock on which the towers stood. One theme runs through the whole complex: remember and experience kinship with the dead.

A different message is embodied by another tribute to those who died on 9/11: the construction of a Navy warship, the *USS New York,* with 7.5 tons of recycled steel from the Twin Towers. Although it was built in Louisiana, the ship was commissioned in ceremonies in the waters off Manhattan on November 7, 2009. Its symbolic crest has an image of the towers and uses the colors of the city departments that first responded to the attacks. Two other ships, the *USS Arlington* and *USS Somerset,* are similar commemorations of those who died at the Pentagon and in a field in Somerset County, Pennsylvania, on that fateful day.

Public memorials like these struggle with the tension between collective remembrance and individual sorrow. The family member who leaves a personal item at the Vietnam Veterans Memorial is laying claim to the particular story of one life ended by conflict, a personal focus that can otherwise be lost in the blur of 58,260 engraved names. The relative who speaks through tears to demand that Ground Zero be treated as a cemetery is advancing his/her own grief over shared commemoration. Public sentiment about a collective loss can shape a memorial message that ill serves the needs of grieving kin.

Figure 7.1
National 9/11 Memorial, "Reflecting Absence"
Photograph courtesy Donald Joralemon.

There are times when personal memorializing overwhelms public priorities, when the grief of those closest to the dead demands our shared attention. A good example comes from the medical world. For many years those who oversaw the gift of cadaver organs for transplantation thought that the family who agreed to the donation ought not be able to contact the recipient directly because demands for intimacy could complicate patients' already difficult adjustment to the reality of having a stranger's organ in their bodies. Organ transplant coordinators mediated any communication between donor families and recipients, and the public recognition of donors was generally cast as a collective thank you rather than an individually identifiable story of altruism. Although exceptions occurred, especially when the story had good public relations potential, usually the deceased donor was known only by age and gender.

Donor families were never satisfied with this arrangement, in part because many of them had agreed to give their brain-dead relative's organs to a stranger in the belief that by doing so, some part of their loved one would live on (Sharp 2006). They wanted to know the recipient; they wanted a connection to the person who had now become a kind of living memorial to their dead kin. And they wanted more direct recognition in the public events that celebrated the accomplishments of organ transplantation. Eventually donor families and recipients found ways, including creative use of the Internet, to circumvent the officials who made direct communication difficult. Unsupervised, sometimes complicated relationships resulted. The United Network for Organ Sharing (UNOS), the organization that manages the organ transplantation system in the United States, ultimately bowed to the pressure and created a donor memorial, names and stories included, at its Richmond, Virginia, headquarters. UNOS also sponsors a website (http://nationaldonormemorial.org), which posts tributes to donors, including a poignant portrait of the deceased, and the suggestion that he/she lives on in the recipient. There is also a biennial National Donor Recognition Ceremony.

Intangible Memorials

When we think of memorials, we tend to think of stone and steel and a nearly infinite variety of smaller physical objects by which the dead are remembered, but it is important to recognize that we also perpetuate the memory of the deceased in less tangible forms. Death notices in newspapers, for example, may be perfunctory recitations of life facts or amusing accounts of eccentricities. Not infrequently an anniversary memorial is published on the occasion of a birth or death date. A more innovative approach was taken by a well-known journalist and humorist who famously filmed his own video obituary, announcing at the start "Hi! I'm Art Buchwald and I just died." The *New York Times* posted the video to the Internet in a feature it called "The Last Word."

The less famous among us can also enjoy Internet immortality with a digital memorial posted to one of the many "virtual graveyards" where family and friends can visit and leave their own testimonials and electronic flowers. There is Memorial2U.com, with a home page sporting a blue sky and passing clouds, and MyCemetery.com, which offers the chance to "connect with those who have left us" via messages and tributes. Connecting with the dead is a two-way street, thanks to posthumous e-mail services like youdeparted.com and mylastemail.com that will deliver a message after you die, creating a self-memorial just a little less dramatic than Art Buchwald's.

An emotionally complicated expression of the use of virtual space for remembering comes not from the United States but from South Vietnam, where the Internet site Nghia Trang Online ("Cemetery Online") offers "tombs" for aborted fetuses. The cultural stigma associated with abortion leaves Vietnamese women no other avenue for the expression of grief associated with the loss of a fetus. They use the site to communicate their remorse directly to the fetus ("Forgive your mother, child!") to ongoing conversations about daily life ("Hello, my dear. Are you scared of the rain from the storm today?") (Heathcote 2014). This is a particularly difficult example of life after death in the world of the Internet; it bears some resemblance to the use of Shinto shrines in Japan to honor aborted fetuses.

Another cottage industry involving the dead has sprouted up around genealogical research. This is an odd practice of remembering because in most instances the ancestors recovered by these investigations are people no living person recalls. Yet more and more amateur genealogists are paying for online services that promise to trace family lines. They search graveyards and baptismal records for lost relatives and sometimes journey to foreign lands when records indicate a country of origin. Filling in a family tree with names and birth and death dates can become an all-consuming task, especially when the past reveals links to saints or scoundrels.

Tragic deaths—by accident, violence, or disease—inspire memorials in the form of named scholarships, legislative initiatives, and medical fundraising campaigns in honor of the deceased. When Candy Lightner's daughter Cari died in 1980 as a result of an accident caused by an intoxicated driver, she founded the group Mothers Against Drunk Driving (MADD), which lobbies for stricter blood alcohol limits and more rigorous enforcement of "driving under the influence" laws. Many states have child protection laws named after the victims of assaults and murders. The nationwide AMBER Alert system, a rapid broadcast response to child abductions, was named after Amber Hagerman, who was kidnapped and killed in 1996 at age nine in Arlington, Texas. Some states replace Amber's name with that of a child from their own region who suffered the same fate (e.g., Georgia uses "Levi's Call").

Medical research on a wide range of serious diseases likewise benefits from survivors wishing to make something positive come from a tragic loss. Probably the best known example is the Christopher and Dana Reeve Foundation, "dedicated to curing spinal cord injury by funding innovative research and improving the quality of life for people living with paralysis through grants, information and advocacy" (www.christopherreeve.org). Smaller-scale funding efforts in memory of people who died of particular diseases have become commonplace thanks to medical advocacy groups, especially those related to the high-profile cancers. Who has not been asked to support a "Walk or Relay for Disease X" in memory of someone who died of that condition?

This seemingly disparate set of memory practices tells us that there is no limit to the amount of cultural energy Americans are prepared to invest in the work of remembering. They also show how the meaning of the lost life can be reconfigured as continuing presence, either as a spirit still connected to the living or as an inspiration for political action or medical research. Each example serves to reconnect the dead to the living, not to deny the death but to preserve the memory of the lost life.

Memorial Morality

Memorials that recall mass death due to intentional acts of murder sometimes demand that we vicariously relive the moment of death, in all its bloody detail, so as to embrace a moral message. The US Holocaust Memorial Museum adopts this approach to remembering. Every detail in the permanent exhibit is intended to make the visitor experience something of the horror of Nazi atrocities against Jews. Identification cards of victims distributed at the start of the tour encourage a sense of direct emotional attachment. Architectural elements recreate the boxcars that transported millions to concentration camps and the aerial walkways that kept Aryans separated from Jews in walled-off ghettos. The material residue of human slaughter—clothes, shoes, documentary photographs—leaves no opportunity for denial. A museum guide quotes Elie Wiesel, the founding chairman of the US Holocaust Memorial Council and Nobel laureate: "For the dead and the living we must bear witness." The museum's mission is not just to remember but to prevent future acts of genocide.

The Oklahoma City National Memorial, which commemorates the lives lost to Timothy J. McVeigh's bomb on April 19, 1996, offers a less obvious moral lesson. Visitors are encouraged to sit on the 168 stone and bronze chairs that represent the dead, including the half-sized seats that stand for the children who were killed. In the museum associated with the memorial the moment of the blast is recreated by playing the tape recording from an administrative hearing that was under way that morning. As the explosion interrupts the proceedings, the lights in the room go out and only panicked voices can be heard. The objective, it seems, is to inveigh against terrorism by making us all feel vulnerable.

Other countries have taken a similar approach to memorials. Japan's Hiroshima Peace Memorial Park commemorates the World War II atomic bombing of that city with an unambiguous anti-nuclear-war message brought home by individual stories of those who died from horrific wounds after the attack. School uniforms, burned and torn, testify to the most innocent of the casualties. Cambodia preserves a former school in the capital city of Phnom Penh that was used as an interrogation center by the brutal Pol Pot regime. The Tuol Sleng Genocide Museum features cabinets filled with the skulls of some of the fifteen thousand prisoners held at the site and some of the torture instruments that were used to extort confessions prior to executions. Like the National Holocaust Memorial Museum's, the message is "never again," but Tuol Sleng is also seen as a repository of evidence to bring the guilty to account for their crimes.

The laudable intention of those who design and fund the museums and symbolic spaces may be to advance peace, to prevent genocide or terrorism, but I wonder about the actual motivation of the spectator. I am certain many visitors go to "bear witness" and to commit to playing some role in the prevention of future atrocities, but I also see a voyeuristic impulse behind the vicarious encounters with horrific deaths these sites encourage. It seems rather like rubbernecking after a gruesome highway accident, watching videos of death-dealing disasters, waiting for the inevitable collision at an auto race, or lining up to see the newest Hollywood slasher movie. The safe position of "witness" permits an experience of death at a distance, some of the pathos without any of the real pain.

Why All This Remembering?

New York Times writer Jack Hitt, commenting on the proliferation of memorials, wrote "The American way of death [has] become a way of life" (Hitt 2002, 6).

We have seen that Americans invest an inordinate—perhaps unprecedented—amount of attention in memorializing the dead. This hardly seems appropriate to a culture that is said to be devoted to denying death. Memorials may take some of the sting away from loss by promising continued connection and preserved memories, but surrounding ourselves with reminders of the departed and building museums dedicated to recreating the moment of death do not seem to be effective ways to avoid thinking about our own mortality. We need to look elsewhere for an explanation of our hyper-memorializing habits.

We go some distance in understanding the cultural purpose of rampant memorializing if we think about monuments and museums as stories we tell ourselves about our past. In nonliterate societies oral tradition bears the burden of transmitting core knowledge from generation to generation. Myths and folktales narrate the past—recent and distant—to celebrate the community's place in the universe, to recount the heroic activities of culture heroes, and to sustain a shared vision of moral behavior to one another and to the gods. Key values and rules of conduct are conveyed through symbol and metaphor. The stories hold the key to a community's sense of itself and play a vital role in perpetuating a common view of the world.

America has its own rich oral traditions that serve the same functions. But we have added to our repertoire of culture narratives an impressive body of "stories" in steel and stone. The memorials that occupy our shared spaces convey the image we want to have of our past and the values we consider central to our common identity. A towering obelisk in Washington serves as a material reminder of our culture hero, George Washington, and his role in our origin story, just as tribal myths recount the exploits of mythic figures whose journeys and trials established the social order for all their descendants. An oversized statue of a sagacious Abraham Lincoln is similarly tied to a narrative of near catastrophe from which another culture hero led us into the light of union and prosperity. A sunken battleship in the waters of Pearl Harbor repeats the narrative of America's triumph over adversity, as does the monument at the site of the World Trade Center. The memorials to Martin Luther King Jr. in Atlanta and Washington, DC, celebrate peaceful resistance against injustice. The Vietnam Veterans Memorial conveys the values of patriotism and sacrifice to country.

Memorials to less notable deaths do the same work of history making but at a more familial level. They are selective renditions of a life, with heavy emphasis on the good works and noble traits of the deceased. In some cases, as with Art Buchwald, the account is self-composed, the dead telling us how they wish to be remembered. For most others the memorial, even if only an epitaph on a gravestone or a newspaper obituary, testifies to the values by which the person is thought to have lived his or her life. The implicit lesson is "live as he or she did."

Using memorials to construct a shared history and to reinforce common values is certainly not unusual in the history of world societies. Grand monuments, often with artistic renditions of great accomplishments and/or dynastic histories, are found in association with the graves of important figures from the earliest complex civilizations. In some cases—the Maya of Mesoamerica and the Moche of ancient Peru are good examples—archaeologists only began to truly understand the iconography of such sites when they realized that real people, not supernatural figures, were frequently the subject of murals and finely painted ceramics. Memorializing the deceased from elite segments of society often contributes to the grander purpose of promoting a favored historical narrative and preferred social values.

If America is not unique in employing memorials to construct a vision of the past and a template for social values in the present, then is there anything that distinguishes the way we remember the dead? I think it is that we have commodified and, to some degree, democratized the act of remembering. For most of human history it was the elite who had the privilege of being memorialized, the edited version of their lives transformed into monumental lessons about the past. Contemporary America has opened the memory gates to average citizens caught by tragedies, soldiers killed in conflicts, stars of stage and screen, accident and crime victims, and just about anyone else who has sufficient disposable income to purchase a statue or publish a memoir. Entrepreneurial efforts have dramatically broadened the options for remembering and, in the process, created thriving memorial enterprises that extend the work of memory to include everything from "ghost bikes" to the "virtual bereavement" of online memorials. Religion professor Candi Cann calls this proliferation of new forms of memorialization the "democratizing [of] grief" (Cann 2014, 138).

The result of all this memorializing is a cacophony of voices in our historical narrative. There are repeating themes, including triumph against adversity, personal courage and sacrifice, and patriotic devotion, but there are also many idiosyncratic threads tied to highly individual life stories. This should come as no surprise given the extraordinary value Americans place on individualism; the unique person is as important after death as in life. It is not, I submit, that "the American way of death has become a way of life," as Jack Hitt would have it, but that the American way of death has become an opportunity for each and every one of us to be remembered. We all want a role in the ongoing American story.

Two questions remain: Will we ever reach the saturation point with memorials, when there is just no more space for another site or act of remembrance?

And does all this remembering contribute to a healthy adjustment to loss, or does it promote continued grief by constant reminder? To the first question we can point to the crowding of the Washington Mall, where little room is left for the next war memorial or the next presidential monument. A similar situation across the Potomac means that more and more restrictive criteria have to be applied to whom may still be buried at Arlington Cemetery. The calendar of national holidays dedicated to remembering major leaders and war veterans has also grown to its limits, which explains efforts to have a Presidents Day to honor all who held that office rather than a proliferation of individual national holidays. There may come a time when we will have to do a selective culling of memorials.

The second question relates to the discussion about the meaning of grief and psychological/psychiatric models of recovery from loss that we reviewed in Chapter 5. We saw that there are at least two recovery models for the experience of loss, one that insists on the detachment from memories of the deceased as the key to healing and the other that calls for a new integration of the dead into the emotional life of survivors. Our predilection for memorials appears to run counter to the former and in sync with the latter. Certainly the proliferation of new memorial forms—tattoos of the deceased, memorial car decals, virtual mourning sites—suggests a popular expression of a desire for continued attachment to the dead. As Cann (2014, 16) puts it, "memorials function as replacements for the body, since we cannot keep the body among us; they must be reinscribed in public space, in material remembrance. . . . The dead will return to haunt us if we do not acknowledge them."

Chapter 8

Dying and Death in America: The Prognosis

The hardest part was the waiting. That, to me, was the most difficult. I wanted it [the transplant] so bad . . . and then I would say to myself, "Good God." I would really feel bad because I was praying for someone to die so I could live. So that right there was difficult for me, you know, because I was [being] selfish. I'd think, God, you know, and now that was the hardest [part].

I met Maria[1] at her family's modest home in a southwestern city. She was twenty-five years old and unmarried at the time we spoke; she had been employed as a teacher's aide before pulmonary hypertension incapacitated her. After six months on a transplant waiting list, Maria received a heart-lung replacement. She recovered from the surgery and was free of rejection episodes for the three years since her transplant. Three powerful daily medications, routine time at a rehabilitation exercise center, and regularly scheduled biopsies kept her in relatively good physical condition, although she had not been able to return to work and struggled with the expenses for her medical care. She knew that her donor had been a twenty-year-old woman mountaineer who died as a result of a climbing accident. During my interview with Maria she reflected with ambivalence on what it meant to anticipate a stranger's death (above quote).

Maria's feelings are common among transplant patients. As the demand for replacement organs continues to outpace the supply, critically ill patients end up waiting excruciatingly long periods for their life-extending surgeries. They know that many of their fellows will die before an appropriate organ becomes available. Some resign themselves to their own death, only to find they have to reconnect with the living when an organ miraculously appears. Others grow resentful of the many families who decline donation requests; one asked, "How can they let me die while their relative's body just rots in the ground?" There can also be a macabre sense of humor among waiting patients. Rain, sleet, or snow that makes driving hazardous is "donor weather" and motorcycle riders are "donors in waiting."

In the Prologue I recounted a do-it-yourself funeral in New Hampshire and indicated that I was drawn by that experience to explore the hypothesis that contemporary America is a death-denying culture. It was the conversations I had with transplant recipients like Maria in the years after that funeral that led me to think that the dilemmas of modern dying and death are less about denial than navigating unchartered territory. There is no cultural precedent for the idea that my life depends on your death because I need your organs. In this concluding chapter I want to revisit the idea of death denial in light of the mortal dilemmas we have considered in this book and then take the pulse of the death discussion in America over the past decade, with an eye to what lies ahead.

Threads

There are some threads running through all or most of the dilemmas we have considered, among the most important being the issue of individual rights. Physician-assisted death is all about the contested limits of an individual's right to orchestrate, with a doctor's help, his/her own demise. The controversies regarding vegetative states center on the question of whether anyone has the right to terminate life-preserving care for another person. Determinations of death based on brain criteria challenge the right of family to insist on the more traditional cardiac definition. Does an individual have a right to mourn without having a medical diagnosis slapped on him/her, and does a living community have rights over the remains of their ancestors? Finally, who has the right to choose which dead are worthy of being memorialized and to decide what form that remembrance should take?

Reflecting on the reasons for America to have become so obsessed by memorialization, the art historian and American studies scholar Erika Doss calls attention to the growth of "rights consciousness" after the tumultuous social movements of the 1960s and 1970s. She says that "today's public sphere has become a 'playing field of citizenship' where rights are asserted and claimed" (Doss 2010, 37). She cites the work of Michael Schudson, a journalist who has written on the evolution of ideas of citizenship in the United States. Schudson argues that rights-conscious citizenship has expanded the authority of the courts as arbitrators of civic conflicts. For Doss, this rights-consciousness has come with a sense of entitlement that drives self-interest groups to assert their priorities in the public sphere, which we have certainly witnessed in the cases reviewed throughout this book. We have also seen a resort to the courts to mediate the disputes that result, as Schudson would predict.

The second thread in our explorations concerns the influence of religiously inspired views in dying and death disputes. From Christian interpretations of life's sanctity in cases of PAD, VS, and brain death to the assertion of Native American spiritual claims on the bones of Kennewick Man/Ancient One, we have seen religious groups as prime players in the contests over dying and death. The rise of the "moral majority" as an influential wing of the Republican Party, beginning with President Reagan's first election, continues today in the political opposition to everything from President Obama's Affordable Care Act (e.g., its support of insurance coverage for birth control services) to resistance to gay rights under the cover of state-based versions of the federal Religious Freedom Restoration Act of 1993. Although court cases in some of the most visible disputes—remember Terri Shiavo—have not necessarily favored their positions, the influence of religious groups on the public debates about dying and death should not be underestimated.

The third connecting theme in the previous chapters concerns the role of biomedicine as an institution that is both shaped by currents in American culture and, in turn, can influence those currents. To see biomedicine as culturally embedded is to adopt a perspective at odds with its practitioners' objectivist presumptions. As Janelle Taylor (2003) puts it, biomedicine is the "culture of no culture," by which she means that it is exactly biomedicine's claim to be free of cultural influence that is the core component of its cultural perspective. The popular idea of cultural competency in medicine, thought to be the solution for miscommunication between doctors and patients, rarely requires that physicians consider the cultural frameworks that *they* bring to the therapeutic encounter: patients have culture; doctors depend on science.

Biomedicine contributes to the dilemmas at the end of life by assuming that the scientific foundation for diagnostic and prognostic judgments trumps the commonsense wisdom that patients and families bring to the bedside. This is most powerfully seen in cases like Jahi McMath, where the medical certainty about brain death ran up against the conviction that a breathing body can't be dead. It is also evident in a family's refusal to accept the hopelessness of a long-term vegetative state. Transforming grief into a pathology based on time and symptom criteria is another example of the widening gap between specialist and lay worldviews that has confounded Americans' experience of death and its aftermath. The same scientific pretention to objective truth is also evident in the contest over Native American bones.

These three threads—rights, religion, and medical/scientific culture—suggest to me that there is more than denial at work in the way contemporary Americans think about and respond to dying and death; the end of life has become an important arena for contests over core beliefs and strongly held values. It is, for example, an oversimplification, if not a distortion, to argue that the Schiavo and McMath parents were denying death when they rejected the medical formulation of personhood implicit in VS and brain death determinations. Brittany Maynard could hardly be accused of denying death as she scheduled the timing of her own demise. The debate about grief as a disease is also hard to see as simply a manifestation of death denial.

Denial?

One could argue that the denial of death is manifest in other aspects of American mortality management. The classic examples include death kept out of sight by institutionalizing the dying, the dead embalmed to make them appear to be simply sleeping, corpses persevered in cryonic suspension, the use of euphemisms for death (e.g., passed on, crossed over), and funeral rituals abbreviated or replaced with memorial services. However, we have seen that there are reasons other than denial for each of these cultural trends. I argue that whatever might have been said about denial in American death customs at the end of the twentieth century no longer holds true. Just as baby boomers have demanded that social and cultural practices be readjusted for earlier stages of their life cycle, so are they bringing death back to center stage as they wrestle with the mortality of their parents and, soon, their own. Let's look at the evidence of a renewed focus on death.

Death Professions

In earlier times the only semiprofessional death experts were the carpenters who fashioned caskets and the clergy who performed funerals. There are now legions of specialists, from those who care for the dying to the armies of grief counselors who stand ready to assist with the emotional toll of death. All of these specialists have professional associations, publications, websites, and regular conferences. For example, the National Association for Home Care and Hospice (www.nahc.org/haa) has an annual conference in different locations across the United States as well as an annual lobbying trip to Washington, DC, to press legislators on end-of-life issues. The Association for Death Education and Counseling (www.adec.org) sponsors continuing education programs, conferences, certificates in thanatology, and a variety of publications. The 37th Annual Conference for the ADEC took place in San Antonio, Texas, in April 2015. The program included a professional development course on Complicated Bereavement and Grief Therapy that promised to "help to identify individuals and families experiencing more complicated, traumatic, prolonged or delayed grief and to acquaint participants with interventions that will ameliorate the concomitant risks to the health, psychosocial adaptation and interpersonal relationships of the bereaved" (Conference Program). This should sound familiar!

Death Academics

The death professions are accompanied by an impressive array of academic subspecialties focused on dying and death. Some are both international and interdisciplinary, like the England-based Association for the Study of Death and Society (www.deathandsociety.org), whereas others are simply a research focus within an academic discipline, such as the Dying and Bereavement Interest Group within the Society for Medical Anthropology (www.medanthro.net/DABIG). There are also organizations that seek to act as a bridge between academic institutions and the wider community, including death professionals. A good example is Columbia University's Seminar on Death (www.columbia.edu/cu/seminars/death). Most of these groups and organizations publish some combination of journals, edited collections, and monographs. Their members are also responsible for many course texts for classes on dying and death, such as Robert J. Kastenbaum's *Death, Society, and Human Experience* (2008), which has gone through many editions.

Deserving special mention are freestanding or university-affiliated bioethics/medical ethics centers or institutes. It is common for the scholars associated with these centers to be called on by the news media for opinions about dying and death controversies. Presidential commissions on bioethics have also drawn heavily from faculty affiliated with the best known of the organizations, like the Hastings Center (www.thehastingscenter.org) and the Kennedy Institute of

Ethics (https://kennedyinstitute.georgetown.edu). The journals they publish, along with the many other outreach media they produce, have had a significant impact on the way the larger public understands dying and death dilemmas.

Some of the academic work on dying and death over the past two decades has been supported by initiatives of nonprofit organizations that want to advance our conversation on mortality. The billionaire George Soros channels much of his philanthropic work through the Open Society Foundations, which funded the nine-year Project on Death in America (1994–2003) with the goal of promoting palliative care and improving other aspects of medicine at the end of life. The Hastings Center, mentioned above as a prominent bioethics institute, has supported projects related to dying, most recently in support of their Guidelines on End-of-Life Care. The Institute of Medicine, the health arm of the nonprofit National Academy of Sciences, has produced two influential reports, Approaching Death: Improving Care at the End of Life (IOM 1997) and Dying in America: Improving Quality and Honoring Individual Preferences Near the End of Life (IOM 2015). The Pew Charitable Trusts funds the Pew Research Center, which has done public opinion polling on many death issues, like that cited in Chapter 2 on PAD (Pew Research Center n.d.). The IOM and Pew reports carry a great deal of weight with media sources and politicians.

Popular Death Literature

The dying memoir is certainly not new to American readers. I still recall the powerful impact that John Gunther's *Death Be Not Proud* (1949) had on my young mind; the account of a seventeen-year-old boy dying of a brain tumor hit close to home because a childhood friend had succumbed to the same condition just before I read the book. But it seems to me that the variety of nonfiction accounts of dying and death has mushroomed in recent years, in no small measure because many of the works have been very popular. In Chapter 1 I mentioned Mitch Albom's *Tuesdays with Morrie* (1997), which was a phenomenal success not only as a book but also as a feature-length film by the same name. I started the chapter on grief with a quote from another recent best-selling death account, Joan Didion's *The Year of Magical Thinking* (2005). I begin my Dying and Death class with a lesser-known but still moving memoir by Douglas Hobbie: *Being Brett: Chronicle of a Daughter's Death* (1996).

It is not just memoires that have proliferated in recent years; explorations of some of the more taboo aspects of death, written by journalists or death professionals, have also gained wide audiences. Science writer Mary Roach reported on all the dark secrets of human cadavers in *Stiff* (2003), the mortuary director and poet Thomas Lynch took us behind the scenes at funeral homes in *The Undertaking* (1997), and the young mortician Caitlin Doughty tells us more than we may have wanted to know about cremation in *Smoke Gets in Your Eyes* (2014).

Physicians have contributed to the burgeoning death literature. Yale surgeon Sherwin B. Nuland made us confront the biological reality of death in the best-selling and National Book Award–winning *How We Die* (1995). The psychiatrist Christine Montross meditates on the power of the medical school anatomy lab in *Body of Work* (2008). Atul Gawande, surgeon and best-selling author, offers lessons from his clinical experience with dying patients and his personal journey with his father's death in *Being Mortal* (2014). Along the same lines, Pauline Chen offers *Final Exam: A Surgeon's Reflections on Mortality* (2007). Add to these books the innumerable articles by physicians on ethical issues in dying and death, and it is clear that the medical profession has had a profound impact on the evolution of America's death debates.

In Chapter 5 I made mention of the expansive self-help literature related to grief, but that genre also includes many titles explaining how to bring spirituality to the process of dying, how to be a good caregiver, and how to plan a funeral for yourself or a loved one. There is also a plethora of sources that promise to direct you through the process of writing a will or other legal documents related to death. Some of these works are authored by professional psychologists and lawyers; others are written by alternative healing specialists or a wide range of self-appointed counselors and advisers.

In the category of popular literature we should also mention the news stories, theme series, opinion pieces, and editorials that appear in national and local newspapers. The *New York Times,* for example, has an index of their death-related coverage (Death and Dying n.d.) that includes commentaries and news stories on death and dying. It published a front-page story in a Sunday edition titled, "Teenagers Face Early Death, on Their Terms" (March 28, 2015); it documented a new effort to encourage terminally ill minors to plan what they want to happen as they near death. My local paper, the *Hampshire Gazette,* published a series of stories (September 2014) about the decision of a ninety-year-old woman to end her life by refusing food and water, which generated so much public response that local hospice leaders organized a community forum to talk about end-of-life choices.

Death in Film and Television

There is no point in belaboring the obvious: death is ubiquitous in movies and television programs and always has been. But I am not so interested in body counts or degrees of realism in death scenes as I am in the cinematic exploration of some of the issues we have covered in previous chapters. For example, in Chapter 1 I referred to Margaret Edson's play-turned movie, *Wit,* and pointed out that it confronts the horror of an isolated medical death that most of us dread. The French film *The Diving Bell and the Butterfly* (Schnabel 2007) adapted to the screen the real story of a forty-three-year-old man who survives a stroke but is left in a "locked-in" condition in which his only means of communication is eye blinks. This award-winning movie recalls the issues of personhood and consciousness that we considered in regard to vegetative states. A number of films have dealt directly with assisted death. The highly acclaimed, Oscar-winning Spanish film *The Sea Inside* (Amenábar 2004) follows the determined effort of a quadriplegic to end his life. Another Oscar-winning film, *The English Patient* (Minghella 1996), ends with a nurse administering a lethal medication at the protagonist's request. For many more films on this theme, see the list compiled by Derek Humphry, the founder of the Hemlock Society (www.finalexit.org/assisted_suicide_in_the_movies.html).

Comedy has been central to screen explorations of the meaning of life and death. The innovative HBO series *Six Feet Under,* which centered on a family-owned funeral home, used humor to consider everything from the experience of sudden death to the mechanics of embalming. It won critical acclaim and ran for five seasons, from 2001 to 2005 (Ball). The irreverent British comedy troop Monty Python offered a disturbing but amusing look at the Grim Reaper's interruption of a rural dinner party in *The Meaning of Life* (Jones 1983). The struggle between biomedicine and death is conveyed in a tragic/comic fashion in a short animated film from Spain, *The Lady and the Reaper* (García 2009).

At the opposite extreme are documentaries designed to both educate about dying and to advocate for reforms of our medical system as it pertains to end-of-life care. Without question, the best example is Bill Moyer's four-part, six-hour-long *On Our Own Terms* (2011), which originally aired on PBS stations across the country and can now be accessed online with supporting educational material. Moyers covers many of the issues raised in this book and does so with powerful personal stories from the dying and those who care for them. Two other notable documentaries, both by the American anthropologist Barbara Myerhoff, are the Academy Award–winning *Number Our Days* (Littman 1976), about a Jewish community center for the elderly in Venice, California, and *In Her Own Time* (Littman 1986), which explores Myerhoff's spiritual search after being diagnosed with terminal lung cancer. Greg Palmer's PBS special, *Death: The Trip of a Lifetime* (1993), explores mourning, grief, and conceptions of the dead across many cultures.

Death on the Web, in Social Media, and in Popular Culture

The Internet has become a fertile ground for experiments and innovations in the management of dying and death. A short list would include dying support groups (especially for the full variety of cancers), alternative medicine sites, virtual memorials and cemeteries, self-help sources for grief, advocacy sites for and against PAD, forums for posting accounts of near-death experiences, and educational sites for everything from cremation to "green burials." Some sites stretch the boundary between private and public. The sports writer Martin Manley developed a website that would posthumously account for his own 2013 suicide outside a Kansas police station (Gross 2013). National Public Radio figure Scott Simon posted tweets from his dying mother's hospital bedside, conveying in 140 characters something of the emotional exchanges between the two of them.

Two Internet experiments, each of which sought to foster greater openness about dying and death, emerged between 2011 and 2013. The first was created by a forty-year-old London-based web designer named Jon Underwood, who adapted an idea from the Swiss sociologist Bernard Crettaz to create a web template for "Death Cafés." Modeled on the tradition of literary salons, the idea was to use social media and other communication means to gather a group of strangers in a local coffee shop to discuss death. The website deathcafe.com offers logistical support and resource materials to help planners organize the events. The objective is "to increase awareness of death with a view to helping people make the most of their (finite) lives" (deathcafe.com/what). As of 2014 there were reported to be many hundreds of these gatherings worldwide, some of which have a regular schedule of meetings.

A culinary alternative to the Death Café was the inspiration of Michael Hebb, a creative restaurateur and social activist based in Portland, Oregon. He and a group of students from the University of Washington developed the idea, "Let's have dinner and talk about death," which subsequently took the form of a website designed to help people organize such events (deathoverdinner.org). As you navigate through the planning process, you are invited to select from lists of provocative articles, videos, and audio files for participants to read and/ or view in advance of the dinner. Hebb gave a talk on the project to a TEDMED gathering in 2013 ("Michael Hebb" 2013).

My own Internet experiment involved providing open access to an earlier version of this manuscript with an associated blog. My goal was to encourage a dialog that I could use as I revised the text. At one point I posted the following:

He Died on Facebook!

It was more than forty years since we had last been in contact, way back in high school in New Jersey. He found and friended me on Facebook, and for the past couple of years I have enjoyed reconnecting and learning about his life. There was sadness—a much beloved wife died young—but also a real passion for family, friends, classic rock and roll, and professional sports. The connection may have been virtual, but it still felt like a renewed relationship.

Then reposts of old pictures began to appear on his wall, followed by expressions of sympathy and mourning. He had suddenly died over the holidays, from a cancer that moved faster than anyone expected. Several people posted as though he were still on the other end and could understand how much he will be missed.

In some cultures the wailing of relatives notifies the community of a death. In others, including an earlier America, carefully crafted—even artful—death notices in the local newspaper did the job. Now it's Facebook. It could be that because I didn't grow up with this avenue of communication, it seems shallow, superficial, minimally sincere. How many seconds are eaten by a comment to a wall post, how much real sympathy is involved? Type and go on with your own life. Is it any better than a death notification in a Tweet? Doesn't this seem to trivialize a passing?

A sixty-year-old social worker and reader of my blog gently chided me. She recalled having a similar cynical response to this use of Facebook but then saw a group of teenagers she was working with use the site to convey important emotions and memories after a friend's death. She ended her thoughtful response by asking, "Who can judge a memorial's legitimacy, after all? Are bouquets at the site of auto accidents or flags flown at half staff more legitimate?"

This experience taught me to take seriously the experimentation found on the Internet around issues of dying and death. In addition to the proliferation of educational material now available online, there is also a stunning amount of energy being invested in creating novel ways for Americans to respond to the challenges of dying, death, and mourning. I am certain we have only seen the beginning of this trend.

Final Thoughts

The serious engagements with the complications of modern dying and death that I have reviewed above are hard to reconcile with the idea that Americans are dedicated to pretending life is eternal and death, in the words of the anthropologist Geoffrey Gorer (1955), pornographic and taboo. The more nuanced view I have adopted in this book is that there are special characteristics of mortality in modern America related to epidemiological shifts, demographic and social patterns, and changing cultural priorities that have challenged traditional views of mortality and its aftermath. The response to these shifting sands is not denial so much as contestation, improvisation, and a good dose of confusion.

Looking forward, what is death's prognosis? I suggest that the baby-boom generation will continue to demand greater attention to end-of-life issues and will bring to the debate the same spirit of innovation and rebellion that has marked its progress through the life course so far. One measure of this trend already well under way is the increasing number of Americans who have completed advance directives or living wills. According to a 2014 report, "the percentage of seniors with living wills . . . increased from 47 percent in 2000 to 72 percent in 2010," although that has not resulted in a change in the numbers of persons who die in hospitals (Preidt 2014).

I argue that physician-assisted death will slowly gain greater acceptance through state-by-state legislative victories and as a result of the force of autonomy as a core value in American culture. However, I see continuing conflict over the treatment of vegetative state patients and in cases of persons declared dead based on the brain definition. Some of those conflicts will rise to the scale of public controversy as a result of the alliances among conservative religious groups and their ability to attract media attention,[2] but far more will ultimately be resolved by better communication between physicians and family members.

I expect that grief will continue down the path to disease status and that new pharmaceuticals promising relief will be directly promoted to an increasingly drug-dependent population. The pressures to streamline mourning and the potential profit for health care providers and drug companies will be far stronger than the forces of resistance to this next step in the medicalization of life. The best-case scenario is for the diagnostic criteria that are ultimately implemented to leave at least some room for the normal response to loss.

Overshadowing developments related to the management of dying will be the increasing cost pressures associated with end-of-life care. We already spend more for medical care in the final months of life than during most of the rest of the life cycle, but this financial burden will spiral right along with the increasing numbers of baby boomers approaching the end of their lives. I expect that at some point cost considerations will come out from behind the screen to be transparently debated as an unfortunate but necessary factor in medical decision making. The result will either be a sensible approach to weighing benefits and costs as dying patients near the point of medical futility or we will see an even greater divergence in the care provided based on the patient's resources. If the latter transpires, there will be a certain irony in the fact that the rich may well suffer more as medicine struggles against the inevitable, whereas the poor may find a more peaceful end in a supportive hospice or at home with loving relatives.

The last of the dilemmas I have considered, related to how we remember our dead, poses more questions than answers when it comes to predicting the future. On the one hand, some of the fervor behind demands for respectful care of the distant dead is tied to the identity politics of our times, which are unlikely to stabilize. On the other hand, the motivation to use memorialization to enlarge the American story is probably guaranteed to continue. The now-instinctive drive to build memory structures to honor the dead after tragedies, be they natural or man-made, is also certain to remain a part of how America remembers.

Disputes over how we manage the end of life and its aftermath reveal important lessons about the cultural divisions that mark American society and give at least some indication of where we are headed. So much has changed in the way we experience dying and death that it should come as no surprise that new ways of managing the process are still very much works in progress. When I consider the conflict-laden landscape of dying and death in America, I don't see denial; I see sincere struggles driven by deep convictions over what responsibility we have to ourselves and our loved ones as life ends.

Notes

Chapter 1

1. This characterization comes from *The Last Passage* by Donald Heinz (1999).
2. The notion of a good death has a long history, often associated with religious conceptions of morality and postmortem judgment (Ariès 1981; Green 2008).
3. The 1993 Family and Medical Leave Act provides for thirteen weeks of unpaid leave for a variety of life events but does not include time off after a death.

Chapter 2

1. As of this writing a court decision permitting physician-assisted death is under appeal in New Mexico.
2. The PEW report showed greater support (66 percent) for the general proposition that a person should, in some situations, be allowed to die. The support for PAD in particular was just under a majority (49 percent).
3. Dr. Atul Gawande's recent book *Being Mortal* (2014) reveals how doctors push treatment beyond the balance point between gain and suffering.
4. Two other European nations, Luxembourg and Belgium, have recently legalized PAD, with varying regulations.
5. The US Supreme Court, in two 1997 cases (*Washington v. Glucksberg* and *Vacco v. Quill*), ruled that there is no constitutional right to PAD.
6. A good review of end-of-life issues raised by advocates for the disabled is Lillie and Werth (2007).
7. Only in 2001 did the Dutch Parliament legally authorize PAD.

Chapter 3

1. A meta-review of PV studies showed that prevalence statistics are quite unreliable due to variations in diagnostic criteria and methods (Van Erp et al. 2014). The statistic cited here is an often repeated figure from the American Academy of Neurology (GDDI 1994).
2. Locked-in syndrome is another disorder of consciousness, but it involves evidence of awareness despite general paralysis and an inability to communicate by ordinary means.

3. Charismatic Catholicism is a movement within the Catholic Church that mirrors Pentecostal worship practices in their intensity and focus on prophetic prayer.

4. US Attorney General Ashcroft threatened Oregon doctors with federal prosecution should they assist patients to die under that state's Death with Dignity law, which permits physician-assisted suicide under strict conditions. On January 18, 2006, the US Supreme Court, in a six-to-three decision, found Oregon's law to be legal and specifically rebuked Ashcroft for overstepping his authority.

5. According to the US Census Bureau, divorce rates in America have been dropping for several years but remain among the highest in comparison to other developed countries (US Census Bureau 2012).

6. Actually a young person in a coma has about a 50 percent chance of regaining consciousness within a two- to three-month time period.

7. The National Hospice and Palliative Care Organization (NHPC) provides web links to the living will forms accepted in each state (www.caringinfo.org/i4a/pages/Index .cfm?pageid=3425). The American Bar Association has a very well-developed set of "tool kits" for drafting these documents (www.abanet.org/aging/toolkit/home.html).

Chapter 4

1. Peter Singer (1994) makes this case on the basis of a review of the committee's files.

2. California's "Medical Injury Compensation Reform Act" was signed into law in 1975. It caps damages for the negligent death of a child at $250,000, an amount that has not been increased since the law was passed.

3. The New Jersey statute requires the application of cardio-pulmonary criteria for a death declaration if the responsible physician is aware of the family's religious objections to the concept of brain death (NJ Declaration of Death Act, N.J. STAT. ANN. 26:6A-3).

4. Shewmon (2001) discounts the integrating function of the brain and the top-down model of coordination of somatic processes.

Chapter 5

1. After climbing to 32.9 percent of births in 2009, the rate of cesarean deliveries has declined modestly in the United States in recent years. It is still nearly one-third of all births and well above the rates in most other developed countries (CDC 2013).

Chapter 6

1. Marge Bruchac called this quote to my attention.

2. NAGPRA defines "cultural affiliation" as "a relationship of shared group identity which can be reasonably traced historically or prehistorically between a present day Indian tribe . . . and an identifiable earlier group."

3. The five colleges are Amherst, Smith, Mount Holyoke, and Hampshire Colleges, and the University of Massachusetts at Amherst.

4. From court filing as reported by Dave Schafer and John Stang, "Anthropologists Fight to Study Kennewick Bones," *Tri-City Herald*, October 18, 1996.

5. The recognition of repatriation is also enshrined in the 2007 UN Declaration on the Rights of Indigenous Peoples in Article 12: "Indigenous peoples have the right to manifest, practice, develop and teach their spiritual and religious traditions, customs and ceremonies; the right to maintain, protect, and have access in privacy to their religious and cultural sites; the rights to the use and control of their ceremonial objects; and the right to the repatriation of their human remains."

Chapter 7

1. A lively debate about the ethics of these displays has asked whether the bodies were acquired with appropriate consent and challenged what it means to turn corpses into aesthetic objects (Linke 2005; Tanassi 2007).

Chapter 8

1. I have changed the name and obscured the home location to provide confidentiality.

2. Although conservative religious groups have had a prominent role to play in these debates, there are other religious traditions that advocate for a more permissive approach to death decisions. The Unitarian Universalists, for example, have a long-standing position in favor of the dying person's right to make his/her own choices at the end of life.

References

Ad Hoc Committee of the Harvard Medical School to Examine the Definition of Brain Death. 1968. "A Definition of Irreversible Coma." *Journal of the American Medical Association* 205: 337–340.

Albom, Mitch. 1997. *Tuesdays with Morrie: An Old Man, a Young Man, and Life's Greatest Lesson.* New York: Doubleday.

Amenábar, Alenandro (director). 2004. *The Sea Inside.* Fine Line Features.

American Medical Association. 1994. "Opinion 2.211—Physician-Assisted Suicide." www.ama-assn.org/ama/pub/physician-resources/medical-ethics/code-medical-ethics/opinion2211.page.

American Psychiatric Association. 2013. *Diagnostic and Statistical Manual,* 5th ed. Washington, DC: American Psychiatric Association.

Ariès, Phillipe. 1981. *At the Hour of Our Death.* New York: Knopf.

Armstrong-Fumero, Fernando. 2014. "Even the Most Careless Observer: Race and Visual Discernment in Physical Anthropology from Samuel Morton to Kennewick Man." *American Studies* 53 (2): 5–30.

Ball, Alan (executive producer). 2001–2005. *Six Feet Under* (television series). Home Box Office.

Bernat, James L. 2014. "Whither Brain Death?" *American Journal of Bioethics* 14: 3–8.

Black, Donald W., and J. E. Grant. 2014. *DSM-5þ Guidebook: The Essential Companion to the Diagnostic and Statistical Manual.* Washington, DC: American Psychiatric Publishing.

Bonelli, R. M., E. H. Prat, and J. Bonelli. 2009. "Philosophical Considerations on Brain Death and the Concept of the Organism as a Whole." *Psychiatria Danubina* 21: 3–8.

Botkin, J. 1988. "Anencephalis Infants as Organ Donors." *Pediatrics* 82: 250–252.

"Brain-Dead Woman Who Gave Birth to Girl Dies." 2005. NBC News. August 3. www.nbcnews.com/id/8801899/ns/health-womens_health/t/brain-dead-woman-who-gave-birth-girl-dies/#.Vgv9iOxViko.

Brody, Howard, L. D. Hermer, L. D. Scott, L.L. Grumbles, J. E. Kutac, and S. McCammon. 2011. "Artificial Nutrition and Hydration: The Evolution of Ethics, Evidence, and Policy." *Journal of General Internal Medicine* 25: 1053–1058.

Bruchac, Margaret M. 2007. "Historical Erasure and Cultural Recovery: Indigenous People in the Connecticut River Valley." PhD diss., University of Massachusetts.

Cann, Candi K. 2014. *Virtual Afterlives: Grieving the Dead in the Twenty-First Century.* Lexington: University Press of Kentucky.

Cassell, Joan. 2005. *Life and Death in Intensive Care.* Philadelphia: Temple University Press.

Centers for Disease Control and Prevention (CDC). 2013. "Births—Method of Delivery." www.cdc.gov/nchs/fastats/delivery.htm.

Chen, Pauline W. 2007. *Final Exam: A Surgeon's Reflections on Mortality.* New York: Alfred A. Knopf.

Conklin, Beth. 2001. *Consuming Grief: Compassionate Cannibalism in an Amazonian Society.* Austin: University of Texas.

"Cruzan's Condition Downgraded to Critical." 1990. *New York Times.* December 26. www.nytimes.com/1990/12/26/us/cruzan-s-condition-downgraded-to-critical.html.

Declaration of Purpose—Asatru Folk Assembly. http://asatrufolkassembly.org/about-the-afa /declaration-of-purpose/.

Daum, Meghan. "Jahi McMath, Alive in Social Media." 2013. Los Angeles Times. December 31. www.latimes.com/opinion/op-ed/la-oe-daum-jahi-brain-dead-20140102-column .html.

"Death and Dying." n.d. *New York Times.* http://topics.nytimes.com/top/news/health/diseases conditionsandhealthtopics/deathanddying/index.html.

"The Death of Nancy Cruzan." 1992. Public Broadcasting Service. March 24. www.pbs.org /wgbh/pages/frontline/programs/transcripts/1014.html.

DeSpelder, Lynne A., and Albert L. Strickland. 2011. *The Last Dance: Encountering Death and Dying,* 9th ed. New York: McGraw Hill.

Dickinson, George E., and Heath C. Hoffmann. 2014. "Roadside Memorials: A 21st Century Development." In *Our Changing Journey to the End: Reshaping Death, Dying, and Grief in America, vol 1: New Paths of Engagement,* edited by Christina Staudt and J. Harold Ellers, 227–252. Santa Barbara, CA: Praeger.

Didion, Joan. 2005. *The Year of Magical Thinking.* New York: Knopf.

Doss, Erika. 2010. *Memorial Mania: Public Feeling in America* Chicago: University of Chicago Press.

Doughty, Caitlin. 2014. *Smoke Gets in Your Eyes: And Other Lessons from the Crematory.* New York: W. W. Norton.

Dunlap, David W. 1991. "Dig Unearths Early Black Burial Ground." *New York Times.* October 9. www.nytimes.com/1991/10/09/nyregion/dig-unearths-early-black-burial-ground .html.

Edson, Margaret. 1999. *Wit.* New York: Dramatists Play Service.

Frances, Allen J. 2012. "DSM 5 to the Barricades on Grief." *Psychology Today.* February 18. www.psychologytoday.com/blog/dsm5-in-distress/201202/dsm-5-the-barricades-grief.

Freud, Sigmund. 1959 [1917]. "Mourning and Melancholia." In *Collected Papers,* vol. 4. New York: Basic Books.

Ganzini L. 2006. "Artificial Nutrition and Hydration at the End of Life: Ethics and Evidence." *Palliative Support Care* 4: 135–143.

García, Javíer Eceio (director). 2009. *Lady and the Reaper.* Green Moon.

Gawande, Atul. 2014. *Being Mortal: Medicine and What Matters in the End.* New York: Metropolitan.

Giacino, J. T., S. Ashwal, N. Childs, R. Cranford, B. Jennett, D. I. Katz, J. P. Kelly et al. 2002. "The Minimally Conscious State: Definition and Diagnostic Criteria." *Neurology* 58: 349–353.

Gorer, Geoffrey. 1955. "The Pornography of Death." *Encounter* (October): 49–52.

Granek, Leeat, and Meghan O'Rourke. 2012. Slate.com. March 12. www.slate.com/articles

/life/grieving/2012/03/complicated_grief_and_the_dsm_the_wrongheaded_move-ment_to_list_mourning_as_a_mental_disorder_.html.

Green, Emma. 2014. "When Patients Are Counting on Miracles." *The Atlantic,* June 18.

Green, James W. 2008. *Beyond the Good Death: The Anthropology of Modern Dying.* Philadel-phia: University of Pennsylvania Press.

Gross, Doug. 2013. "The Sportswriter Who Blogged His Suicide." August 23. www.cnn.com/2013/08/23/tech/web/martin-manley-suicide-website/index.html?hpt=hp_c2.

Guideline Development, Dissemination and Implementations (GDDI) Subcommittee. 1994. "Practice Parameters: Assessment and Management of Patients in the Persistent Vegeta-tive State." *American Academy of Neurology.*

Gunther, John. 1949. *Death Be Not Proud: A Memoir.* New York: Harper.

Harris Polls. 2014. "Most Americans Agree with Right-to-Die Movement." December 5. www.harrisinteractive.com/NewsRoom/HarrisPolls/tabid/447/ctl/ReadCustom%20Default/mid/1508/ArticleId/1531/Default.aspx.

Heathcote, Anthony. 2014. "A Grief That Cannot Be Shared: Continuing Relationships with Aborted Fetuses in Contemporary Vietnam." *Thanatos* 3: 29–45.

Heinz, Donald. 1999. *The Last Passage: Recovering a Death of Our Own.* New York: Oxford University Press.

"Hi-Tech Tombstone Sales Are Slow Going." 2007. CBSNews. December 10. www.cbsnews.com/news/hi-tech-tombstone-sales-are-slow-going.

Hitt, James. 2002. "The American Way of Death Becomes America's Way of Life." *New York Times,* August 18, sec. 4.

Hobbie, Douglas. 1996. *Being Brett: Chronical of a Daughter's Death.* New York: Henry Holt.

Holland, Jason M., Robert A. Neimeyer, Paul A. Boelen, and Holly G. Prigerson. 2009. "The Underlying Structure of Grief: A Taxometric Investigation of Prolonged and Normal Reactions to Loss." *Journal of Psychopathology and Behavioral Assessment* 31: 190–201.

Holloway, Karla F. C. 2002. *Passed On: African American Mourning Stories: A Memorial.* Dur-ham, NC: Duke University Press.

Humphry, Derek. 1991. *Final Exit: The Practicalities of Self-Deliverance and Assisted Suicide for the Dying.* Seacaucus, NJ: Carol Publishing.

Institute of Medicine (IOM). 1997. *Approaching Death: Improving Care at the End of Life.* Washington, DC: The National Academies Press.

Institute of Medicine (IOM). 2015. *Dying in America: Improving Quality and Honoring Indi-vidual Preferences Near the End of Life.* Washington, DC: The National Academies Press.

Iserson, Kenneth V. 1994. *Death to Dust: What Happens to Dead Bodies.* Tucson, AZ: Galen Press.

Jacobs, Elizabeth, I. Rolle, C. E. Ferrans, E. E. Whitaker, and R. B. Warnecke. 2006. "Un-derstanding African Americans' Views of the Trustworthiness of Physicians." *Journal of General Internal Medicine* 21: 642–647.

James, Susan Donaldson. 2014. "Arizona College Student Bounces Back from the Dead After Nearly Giving Organs." ABCNews. May 16. http://abcnews.go.com/Health/arizona-college-student-bounces-back-dead/story?id=23732120.

Jennett, Bryan. 2002. *Vegetative State: Medical Facts, Ethical and Legal Dilemmas.* Cambridge: Cambridge University Press.

Jones, Terry (director). 1983. *Monty Python's Meaning of Life.* Universal Pictures.

Joralemon, Donald. 2002. "Reading Futility: Anthropological Reflections on a Bioethical Concept." *Cambridge Quarterly of Health Care Ethics* 11: 127–133.

Kastenbaum, Robert J. 2008. *Death, Society, and Human Experience,* 8th ed. New York: Pearson.

Kauffman, Jeffrey. 2008. "What Is "Recovery?" *Death Studies* 32: 76.

Kübler-Ross, Elizabeth. 1969. *On Death and Dying.* New York: Macmillan.

"Legal Implications." 2006. 123HelpMe.com. www.123helpme.com/view.asp?id=35726.

"Leverett Neighborhood Wrestles with Weight of a Cross." 2008. *Daily Hampshire Gazette.* June 24.

Lillie, Timothy, and James L. Werth, Jr., eds. 2007. *End of Life Issues and Persons with Disabilities.* Austin, TX: PRO-ED.

Limp, W. Frederick, and Jerome C. Rose. 1986. "The Relocation of the Historical Cemetery at Cedar Grove." *Public Archaeology Forum*: 339–345.

Lindemann, Erich. 1944. "The Symptomatology and Management of Acute Grief." *American Journal of Psychiatry* 101: 141–148.

Linke, Uli. 2005. "Touching the Corpse: The Unmaking of Memory in the Body Museum." *Anthropology Today* 21: 13–19.

Littman, Lynne (director). 1976. *Number Our Days.* Direct Cinema Limited.

Littman, Lynne (director). 1985. *In Her Own Time.* Direct Cinema Limited.

Lock, Margaret. 2002. *Twice Dead: Organ Transplantation and the Reinvention of Death.* Berkeley: University of California Press.

Loomis, Frederick B. 1915. "Edward Hitchcock and the Amherst Indian Collection." *Amherst Graduates' Quarterly,* June.

Lynch, Thomas. 1997. *The Undertaking: Life Studies from the Dismal Trade.* New York: W. W. Norton.

Macdonald, Robert R. 1992. "Bad Blood at the Burial Ground." *New York Times.* September 12. www.nytimes.com/1992/09/12/opinion/bad-blood-at-the-burial-ground.html.

Maercker, Andreas, and Axel Perkonigg. 2013. "Applying an International Perspective in Defining PTSD and Related Disorders: Comment on Friedman." *Journal of Traumatic Stress* 26: 560–562.

Maynard, Brittany. 2014. "My Right to Death with Dignity at 29." CNN. November 2. www.cnn.com/2014/10/07/opinion/maynard-assisted-suicide-cancer-dignity/index.html.

"Michael Hebb: Let's Have Dinner and Talk About Death." 2013. YouTube.com. June 29. www.youtube.com/watch?v=4DT0aMfFtuw.

Minghella, Anthony (director). 1996. *The English Patient.* Miramax Films.

Montross, Christine. 2008. *Body of Work: Meditations on Mortality from the Human Anatomy Lab.* New York: Penguin.

Moyers, Bill D. (director). 2011. *On Our Own Terms: Moyers on Dying.* Public Broadcasting Service.

Multi-Society Task Force on PVS. 1994. "Medical Aspects of the Persistent Vegetative State." *New England Journal of Medicine* 330: 1499–1508.

Muñoz, Erick. 2015. "Plaintiff's Original Petition for Declaratory Judgement and Application for Unopposed Expedited Relief." Tarrant County Court, January 27. www.biodiritto.org/index.php/item/download/449_6456f03baa8b7fcd7c334e009737d7ce.

Murphy, Robert. 1987. *The Body Silent.* New York: Norton.

"National Register Criteria for Evaluation." n.d. National Register Bulletin. www.nps.gov/nr/publications/bulletins/nrb15/nrb15_2.htm.

Nuland, Sherwin. 1995. *How We Die: Reflections of Life's Final Chapter.* New York: Vintage.

Palmer, Greg (director). 1993. *Death: The Trip of a Lifetime.* Public Broadcasting Service.

Peterson, Andrew, L. Norton, L. Naci, A. M. Owen, and C. Weijer. 2014. "Toward a Science of Brain Death." *American Journal of Bioethics* 14: 29–31.

Pew Research Center. n.d. Death and Dying. www.pewresearch.org/topics/death-and-dying.

Pew Research Center. 2006. "Strong Public Support for Right to Die." January 5. www .people-press.org/2006/01/05/strong-public-support-for-right-to-die.

Pew Research Center. 2013a. "Chapter 1: Opinion About Laws on Doctor-Assisted Suicide." November 21. www.pewforum.org/2013/11/21/chapter-1-opinion-about-laws-on-doctor-assisted-suicide.

Pew Research Center. 2013b. "Views on End-of-Life Medical Treatments." November 21. www.pewforum.org/2013/11/21/views-on-end-of-life-medical-treatments.

Pfister, Bonnie. 2005. "Remembering Karen Ann Quinlan." *Post Star*. September 4. http: //poststar.com/lifestyles/remembering-karen-ann-quinlan/article_460ce9dc-8b9e-5778-96b3-1d53d684e46a.html.

Plets, Gertijan, N. Konstantinov, V. Soenov, and E. Robinson. 2013. "Repatriation, Doxa, and Contested Heritages: The Return of the Altai Princess in an International Perspective." *Anthropology and Archeology of Eurasia* 52: 73–100.

Preidt, Robert. 2014. "Nearly Three-Quarters of U.S. Seniors Have Living Wills." *U.S. News and World Report, Health,* April 2.

President's Council on Bioethics (US). 2008. *Controversies in the Determination of Death: A White Paper of the President's Council on Bioethics.* Washington, DC: President's Council on Bioethics.

Prigerson, Holly G., M. J. Horowitz, S. C. Jacobs, C. M. Parkes, M. Aslan, K. Goodkin, B. Raphael et al. 2009. "Prolonged Grief Disorder: Psychometric Validation of Criteria Proposed for DSM-V and ICD-11." *PLoS Medicine* 6(8): e1000121.

Quill, Timothy, and Jane Greenlaw. 2008. "Physician-Assisted Death." In *From Birth to Death and Bench to Clinic: The Hastings Center Bioethics Briefing Book for Journalists, Policymakers, and Campaigns,* edited by Mary Crowley, 137–142. Garrison, NY: The Hastings Center.

Roach, Mary. 2003. *Stiff: The Curious Lives of Human Cadavers.* New York: W. W. Norton.

Rosaldo, Renato. 1988. "Grief and a Headhunter's Rage: On the Cultural Force of Emotions." In *Text, Play, and Story: The Construction and Reconstruction of Self and Society,* edited by Edward M. Bruner, 178–195. Prospect Heights, IL: Waveland Press.

Schnabel, Julian (director). 2007. *The Diving Bell and the Butterfly.* Miramax Films.

Shah, Seema K. 2015. "Piercing the Veil: The Limits of Brain Death as a Legal Fiction." *University of Michigan Journal of Law Reform* 48: 301–346.

Sharp, Leslie A. 2006. *Strange Harvest: Organ Transplantation, Denatured Bodies, and the Transformed Self.* Berkeley: University of California.

Shear, M. Katherine, Naomi Simon, Melanie Wall, Sidney Zisook, Robert Neimeyer, Naihua Duan, Charles Reynolds et al. 2011. "Complicated Grief and Related Bereavement Issues for DSM-5." *Depression and Anxiety* 28(2): 103–117.

Shewmon, D. Alan. 2001. "The Brain and Somatic Integration." *Journal of Medicine and Philosophy* 26: 457, 467–469.

Singer, Peter. 1994. *Death: The Collapse of Our Traditional Ethics.* New York: St. Martin's Press.

Staudt, C., and J. H. Ellens, eds. 2014. *Our Changing Journey to the End: Reshaping Death, Dying, and Grief in America.* Oxford: Praeger.

Svanevik, Michael, and Shirley Burgett. 1995. *City of Souls.* San Francisco: Custom and Limited Editions.

Tanassi, Lucia M. 2007. "Responsibility and Provenance of Human Remains." *American Journal of Bioethics* 7: 36–38.

Taylor, Janelle S. 2003. "Confronting 'Culture' in Medicine's 'Culture of No Culture.'" *Academic Medicine* 78:555–559.

The Terry Wallis Fund. n.d. www.theterrywallisfund.org.

Truog, Robert D., and F. G. Miller. 2014. "Changing the Conversation About Brain Death." *American Journal of Bioethics* 14: 9–14.

"The Unparalleled Success." n.d. Body Worlds. www.bodyworlds.com/en/exhibitions/unparalleled_success.html,

US Census Bureau. 2012. International Statistics. www.census.gov/compendia/statab/cats/international_statistics.html.

US Office of Personnel Management (USOPM). n.d. "Pay & Leave." www.opm.gov/policy-data-oversight/pay-leave/leave-administration/fact-sheets/sick-leave-for-family-care-or-bereavement-purposes.

Van Erp, W. S., J. C. M. Lavrijsen, F. A. van de Laar, P. E. Vos, S. Laureys, and R. T. C. M. Koopmans. 2014. "The Vegetative State/Unresponsive Wakefulness Syndrome: A Systematic Review of Prevalence Studies." *European Journal of Neurology* 21: 1361–1368.

Vries, Lloyd. 2005. "Terri Schiavo Bill Becomes Law." CBSNews. March 21. www.cbsnews.com/news/terri-schiavo-bill-becomes-law.

Walter, Tony. 1996. "A New Model of Grief: Bereavement and Biography." *Mortality* 1: 7–25.

Weiner, Annette B. 1988. *The Trobrianders of Papua New Guinea.* New York: Holt, Rinehart and Winston.

Weir, R. F., and L. Gostin. 1990. "Decisions to Abate Life-Sustaining Treatment for Nonautonomous Patients: Ethical Standards and Legal Liability for Physicians after Cruzan." *Journal of the American Medical Association* 264: 1846–1853.

Wikan, U. 1990. *Managing Turbulent Hearts: A Balinese Formula for Living.* Chicago: University of Chicago Press.

World Health Organization. n.d. "Internal Classifications of Diseases (ICD)." www.who.int/classifications/icd/en.

Zbarsky, I., and S. Hutchinson. 1998. *Lenin's Embalmers.* Translated by B. Bray. London: Harvill.

Index

About the Author

Donald Joralemon earned his doctorate in cultural anthropology from UCLA and has taught at Smith College since 1983. His first book, on Peruvian shamanism, led to an appearance on the National Geographic television channel's program "Taboo" (on "Altered States"). For the last ten years he has done research on the developed world's healing technologies, especially organ transplantation, and published articles in various anthropology and medical ethics journals. He has been interviewed by the *Philadelphia Inquirer* and the *Canadian Medical Journal* and was invited to submit an editorial to *Proto*, the journal for the Massachusetts General Hospital. He is also the author of the widely used textbook *Exploring Medical Anthropology*, now in its third edition.